S. Hrg. 114–68

ENDING MODERN SLAVERY

HEARINGS

BEFORE THE

COMMITTEE ON FOREIGN RELATIONS UNITED STATES SENATE

ONE HUNDRED FOURTEENTH CONGRESS

FIRST SESSION

FEBRUARY 4 AND FEBRUARY 11, 2015

Printed for the use of the Committee on Foreign Relations

Available via the World Wide Web: http://www.gpo.gov/fdsys/

U.S. GOVERNMENT PUBLISHING OFFICE

96–256 PDF   WASHINGTON : 2015

For sale by the Superintendent of Documents, U.S. Government Publishing Office
Internet: bookstore.gpo.gov   Phone: toll free (866) 512–1800; DC area (202) 512–1800
Fax: (202) 512–2104   Mail: Stop IDCC, Washington, DC 20402–0001

(II)

CONTENTS

Wednesday, February 4, 2015

ENDING MODERN SLAVERY: WHAT IS THE BEST WAY FORWARD?

Wednesday, February 11, 2015

ENDING MODERN DAY SLAVERY: THE ROLE OF U.S. LEADERSHIP

ENDING MODERN SLAVERY: WHAT IS THE BEST WAY FORWARD?

WEDNESDAY, FEBRUARY 4, 2015

U.S. SENATE,
COMMITTEE ON FOREIGN RELATIONS,
Washington, DC.

The committee met, pursuant to notice, at 9:35 a.m., in room SD–419, Dirksen Senate Office Building, Hon. Bob Corker (chairman of the committee) presiding.

Present: Senators Corker, Risch, Rubio, Johnson, Flake, Gardner, Isakson, Menendez, Cardin, Shaheen, Coons, and Kaine.

OPENING STATEMENT OF HON. BOB CORKER, U.S. SENATOR FROM TENNESSEE

The CHAIRMAN. The Foreign Relations Committee will now come to order. We have convened this hearing to examine modern slavery and what is being done about it. We recognize that the United States Congress and our executive agencies have worked hard to draw attention to and address modern slavery, but I believe we have come to a point where we can do more. We need to take these efforts to the next level.

I think most Americans would be stunned to know that slavery still exists in this world. Let me pause to state that again. It is difficult to imagine that in this modern day, more than 27 million around the world are forced to live as slaves. At this hearing, in addition to our expert witnesses, we will hear from two individuals who suffered and ultimately escaped this experience, and went on to help others. And we thank them for being with us today.

Modern forms of slavery thrive where the rule of law is weakest. Corruption, crime, and cultural attitudes contribute to a climate of low risk and impunity for those who profit from modern slavery. In many instances, modern slavery is a crime of opportunity for perpetrators. It is often practiced quite openly, for example, in brick or rug manufacturing or in bars or brothels.

Under U.S. law, such conditions are defined as the most severe forms of trafficking in persons, including forced sexual servitude of minors and adults and persons in bonded and other forced labor conditions. Women, children, and men alike are subjected to involuntary labor or sexual exploitation. According to a leading nongovernmental organization, forced labor accounts for 74 percent of victims, and forced sexual servitude accounts for 26 percent of victims. Women and girls are especially vulnerable, accounting for 54 percent of victims. Children under the age of 18 account for 26 percent of victims.

(1)

We have been to countries and met with people who have survived this horrific experience, and heard from people who work to end modern slavery. U.S. Government and private philanthropic funding are spurring increasingly sophisticated efforts to combat modern slavery. There is a growing consensus that in order to end the practice of modern slavery, reliable baseline data and consistent and effective monitoring and evaluation are needed to deal with this issue. Leveraging and coordinating private and government funding are also seen as key challenges by many in the anti-modern slavery community.

Today we will explore these questions to help inform our thinking on how we can maximize our efforts and take them to the next level, and to find the best way forward to begin the process in earnest of putting an end to modern slavery. With that, I turn to our distinguished ranking member, Bob Menendez.

OPENING STATEMENT OF HON. ROBERT MENENDEZ, U.S. SENATOR FROM NEW JERSEY

Senator MENENDEZ. Thank you, Mr. Chairman, and thanks for calling a very important hearing. Human trafficking in the form of sexual exploitation, forced labor, forced marriage, debt bondage, and the sale and exploitation of children is one of the greatest moral challenges of our time. And the numbers are staggering.

As we speak, there are 50 million refugees and displaced people in the world, the largest number since World War II. All are at risk of exploitation, and some will fall victim to human trafficking. This is not a new phenomenon, but there are new, more sinister factors exacerbating it. With the growth of transnational organized crime, the rise of brutal nihilistic groups, like ISIL and Boko Haram, and sectarian violence forcing millions to flee their homes.

The International Labor Organization estimates that there are at least 21 million victims of human trafficking in the world. Over 5 million of them are children. It is estimated that forced labor alone generates $150-plus billion in profits annually, making it the second-largest income source for international criminals next to the drug trade, making it obscenely lucrative for unscrupulous labor brokers to induce people to cross borders, thinking that they are going for legal work, only to trap them in labor or sexual exploitation.

NGOs and civil society have been doing what they can to combat human trafficking, and business and governments should do more to help. Governments can muster more political will, companies can clean up their supply chains and make that information public, and the public can be more aware of who picks the fruit on their breakfast cereal in the morning, or who slaved in the sweatshop to sell the shirt on their back. This hearing helps raise that awareness.

And with that, Mr. Chairman, I will look forward to working with you in the coming months on a bipartisan approach to ending every form of human trafficking around the world.

The CHAIRMAN. Thank you, and I want to thank others for being here. We will now turn to our witnesses, and we appreciate the tremendous commitment that they have shown in this effort.

Our first witness is Gary Haugen, the founder and president of International Justice Mission, IJM, a global organization that protects the poor from violence by partnering with local authorities to rescue victims, bring criminals to justice, restore survivors, and strengthen justice systems. IJM combats modern slavery, sex trafficking, rape, police brutality, property grabbing, and other forms of violence in Africa, Latin America, South Asia, Southeast Asia.

Before founding IJM, he served as the director of the U.N. investigation of the aftermath of the Rwandan genocide, and as a human rights attorney for the U.S. Department of Justice. He has been recognized by the U.S. State Department as a trafficking in persons hero. I have gotten to know him personally, and he certainly deserves that recognition.

Our second witness is Shawna Bader-Blau. I am going to call you ''Shawna'' if that is okay. [Laughter.]

Shawna is the executive director of the Solidarity Center in Washington, DC, the largest global worker rights organization in the United States. Solidarity Center works with partners and allies from more than 400 unions, nongovernmental organizations, legal aid groups, and human rights defenders from around the world to help workers exercise their rights and improve their working conditions.

Prior to her appointment as executive director, she served as the Solidarity Center's regional program director for the Middle East and North Africa, where she worked directly with victims of forced labor and human trafficking, and with labor activists and human rights defenders.

Thank you for being here and for sharing your thoughts and viewpoints today. We would like to remind you that your full testimony, full statements will be included in the record without objection. So if you could please keep your remarks to about 5 minutes, we would appreciate it so members can engage you in questions. And with that, Mr. Haugen, if you would begin, we would appreciate it.

STATEMENT OF GARY HAUGEN, PRESIDENT, INTERNATIONAL JUSTICE MISSION, ARLINGTON, VA

Mr. HAUGEN. Thank you, Mr. Chairman, and thank you very much for your extraordinary leadership in convening this hearing. I would just like to say that I know that you, the Senators who are on this committee have before you a whole world of threats and crises, and it is a fair question as to whether modern day slavery actually merits this kind of attention today. As the leader of what is now the world's largest antislavery organization, I just want to assure you of three things. Number one, slavery is as brutal as ever. Number two, it is more vast than ever, but also, thirdly, it is more stoppable than ever.

So, first, it is more brutal than ever, and it is as brutal as it has ever been because violence is still at the core of slavery. Whatever you might have seen of 19th century slavery in the movie ''12 Years a Slave,'' those horrible scenes still take place today. In the case files of International Justice Mission, we have murders, mutilations, kidnappings, rapes, torture. It is brutally violent. A couple of our clients just recently had their hands chopped off because they ran away from their traffickers.

So it is as brutal as it has ever been, but surprisingly it is vaster than it has ever been. I think the best estimates on the numbers come from the Global Slavery Index, which put slavery at more than 35 million, which is three times larger than all the slaves extracted from Africa during 400 years of the transatlantic slave trade.

But thirdly, it is more stoppable than at any time in human history. So why is that? For two basic reasons. Number one, throughout all of human history, slavery was really the centerpiece of global economies, and it was perfectly legal, but these things are no longer true. Free market labor has prevailed as the dominant model, and slavery is now against the law. These massive twin battles have been won, and now it is really just for us to finish the job.

I think there actually is a best way forward, but to go forward we have to be clear, I think, about one thing. And that is the answer to the question of why there is so much slavery in the world today is surprisingly simple. Slavery exists on a massive scale in the world today because there are huge swathes of the world where people just do not get in trouble for enslaving other people. In other words, while there are laws against slavery in every country, there are countries in which these laws are virtually completely unenforced. In South Asia, for instance, if you enslave a poor person, you are more likely to be struck by lightning than you are to actually go to prison for that crime.

What the world has to understand about slavery is that it exists on a vast scale for only one reason, and that is impunity. Now, to be clear, impunity is not the only reason why slavery exists. It is the only reason it exists on a vast scale. Slavery exists in developed countries like the United States where actual laws are reasonably well enforced. Even here we can and need to do better because slavery on any scale is unacceptable, right?

But impunity is not the chief explanation why tens of thousands here in the United States are in slavery in our country. It is a more complicated phenomenon. But impunity is the reason why tens of millions are in slavery in our world. And this, Senators, is actually good news. Why? Because impunity can end, and it turns out that when impunity ends, the vast majority of slavery simply goes away. Why is that? Because the vast majority of slavery is soft crime. It is what we call crime of opportunity. You do this because you can. If you can get away with it, you enslave another person because you can make a lot of money off of it. But if you are seriously afraid of going to jail for that, you do not see it as an easy way to make money, and you stop doing it.

Another way to explain this is to say that slavery is, as the chairman said, a crime of opportunity, which means it is highly responsive to risk. Not all crime is like this, but slavery is, and when there is zero risk, it takes place at a very high level. But by contrast, crimes of severe social deviance, for instance, like pedophilia, they take place at a low level, but they are not very responsive to risk because it is compulsive behavior. The perpetrators feel like they have to keep doing it, and it does not respond even when the risk rises.

Similarly, crimes of desperation. You are hungry, and you have to steal bread because you think your family has to survive on that. This is more common, and it is a little bit more responsive to risk. But still it is not that responsive because you feel you have to do it to survive. Crimes of opportunity are totally different, especially a discretionary economic crime like slavery. Crime of opportunity is highly responsive to risk and drops off all together when risk becomes significant. At IJM, we have actually been able to prove this to be true and quantitatively have measured it. We have measured trafficking fall off by as much as 79 percent when impunity ended.

So then, the question becomes, in countries where slavery is thriving, is it possible to fix broken law enforcement so it actually enforces the law? At IJM, we have also proven that this is possible. In countries that even have appalling track records of poor law enforcement, we have proven that it is possible to set up vetted police units that do a great job, fast track courts that bring convictions, and we see the slavery measurably decrease. This is really hard to do, and it takes a deep commitment, but it is absolutely possible.

Finally, I would like to say that many times the world gets confused about fighting slavery because almost all slaves are poor. And thus we assume that we have to eliminate poverty and ignorance in order to be able to end slavery. As a result we either give up on it because that seems impossible, or we try to harden poor people against slavery by ending their poverty and their lack of awareness. In fact, we have spent vast sums on this approach, but it has never measurably reduced slavery. Why is that? Because the traffickers simply move on to an almost infinite supply of 2½ billion other poor people who are still desperate and unaware of the threats and of the schemes, and so the traffickers will go wherever they need to go to find them.

We should, of course, continue to reduce vulnerability by reducing poverty and raising awareness. Of course. But these strategies cannot hope to prevail as long as there is an ocean of impunity. Think of malaria, for instance. Ninety percent of all malaria deaths occur amongst the poor, and so you can think, well, we cannot solve malaria until we solve poverty. In fact, you just need to stop the mosquito from biting the poor person, and it turns out you do not have to wait for poverty to end in order to dramatically reduce malaria. Likewise, rather than trying to end slavery by ending poverty, which we should do for other reasons in any event, it has proven to be so much faster, cheaper, and more effective to get the traffickers to simply stop even trying to enslave others because they are afraid of going to jail.

I believe it is possible like never before in history for the United States to lead in a way that is decisive in the fight against slavery by helping stand up and support a pooled fund that will combine public, private, and philanthropic resources that focus specifically on ending impunity and making sure that those who are poor are not vulnerable. Because here is what we have learned: that traffickers are not brave. And currently they walk around in countries where they are as fearful of going to jail for slavery as they are of being struck by lightning. And as long as that is the case, slavery will continue. But I believe U.S. leadership can change that, and when it does, then slavery will finally be swept into the dustbin of history where it belongs.

Mr. Chairman, thank you very much.

[The prepared statement of Mr. Haugen follows:]

PREPARED STATEMENT OF GARY HAUGEN

Thank you for this opportunity to testify, Chairman Corker. My name is Gary Haugen, and I am the president of International Justice Mission (IJM). We are grateful that you have chosen to make the issue of global slavery one of your top priorities.

As you know, slavery is a crime that inflicts great suffering on tens of millions of victims every year. It takes many forms, including forced sexual exploitation, exploitative labor, domestic servitude, and debt bondage. But all forms of slavery, past and present, share certain characteristics.

First, slavery is unspeakably violent. Over the past 15 years, International Justice Mission has investigated thousands of cases of slavery and worked with local authorities to rescue tens of thousands of children, men, and women. In virtually every case, perpetrators use violence and the threat of violence to terrorize victims into submission and servitude. IJM's clients have experienced kidnapping, brutal beatings, sexual assault and gang rape, mutilation, humiliation, and starvation. Many of our clients report that slaveowners and managers will go to great lengths to track down escaped slaves and bring them back to the facility to be beaten or whipped in front of the other slaves to sow terror and docility.

Second, slavery is an economically motivated crime. This orgy of violence and abuse that factory managers, labor recruiters, brothel owners, and crew bosses inflict on the vulnerable is for a very specific purpose. It is for the purpose of generating profits for the abusers. The simple economic model of reducing labor costs to virtually nothing by coercing labor generates upward of $150 billion in profits.

A conversation between my staff and a Ghanaian slaveowner illustrates this simple calculation. IJM's team was conducting a prevalence study of child labor slavery on Lake Volta in Ghana recently. The team asked a fisherman who had several young child slaves on his boat why he didn't use older children for the dangerous and back-breaking work. He answered without hesitation: "Older kids eat too much. And they start to have their own ideas. The young kids are much easier to control."

A third common characteristic of present day and historic slavery is that in all cases there is a perpetrator. Human beings do not naturally or willingly offer up their bodies and their labor for the abusive enrichment of another. In all cases, slavery occurs when vulnerable people are preyed upon by others possessing slightly more power than they do. Vulnerability alone does not enslave; it requires an enslaver.

One characteristic that modern day slavery does not share with historic slavery is its legal status. During the 400 years of the transatlantic slave trade, slavery was legal. It was legal in the United States from earliest Colonial days to its legal abolition in 1865. Today, in contrast, slavery is legal virtually nowhere in the world. Yet there are more human beings in slavery today than at any previous time in history.

The first half of the abolition agenda—outlawing the crime of slavery has been accomplished. The second half of the abolition agenda—making these laws meaningful to slavery's victims—has barely been attempted.

According to the latest State Department Trafficking in Persons Report, the governments of the three countries reported to have the most number of slaves (totaling over 19.5 million, or over half the world's slaves) reported zero convictions in antitrafficking cases in 2013. Zero.

The obvious question for the committee is this: Why are laws against slavery so seldom enforced?

In our work, IJM has found that antislavery or antitrafficking laws are not enforced because the victims are poor and powerless and have little access to judicial institutions. Perpetrators, in contrast, frequently have ties to local authorities. In some cases, local police are paid by local traffickers to look the other way or are actively complicit in the crime. The overwhelming failure of effective law enforcement against trafficking and slavery has persuaded many policymakers that it is simply impossible for police to change. They have simply given up on the dream of making the protection of law real for poor people. Thus the bulk of U.S. antitrafficking assistance is for programs to prevent the crime by making the victim less vulnerable. Tens of millions of dollars have been spent in public education programs to teach poor communities about the risks of trafficking and slavery.

Hundreds of millions of dollars are spent on education, health, and job creation in hopes of insulating potential victims from exploitation and abuse.

Education, health, and income generation programs are valuable in their own right. But these funds have not had a measurable impact on slavery. Why? Because they do not affect the behavior of the central player in every situation of enslavement and exploitation: the perpetrator. Perpetrators of trafficking, slavery, and debt bondage, whether they are unscrupulous labor recruiters in Qatar, brothel owners in Southeast Asia, or pimps in the United States have one thing in common. They are making money from the subjugation of others. If they are not at risk for going to jail for their crime, they will go to whatever village, slum, city, or state in the world to find the poor and the vulnerable. But they will stop even trying to enslave the poor if they are afraid of going to jail.

Consider Ghana, a lower middle income, democratic nation that has had robust economic growth for the past 5 years. Ghana is a favored partner of the World Bank, whose current grants, loans, and credits total $3.49 billion. The U.S. Government is a generous donor, as well, providing $154 million for health and development last year.

But a third of Ghana's children work, and neither economic growth nor foreign assistance protects thousands of them from actual enslavement in fishing, domestic servitude, artisanal gold mining, begging, and prostitution. Prevalence studies conducted by International Justice Mission (IJM) on Lake Volta over the past 18 months revealed that 60 percent of the children fishing on the lake were clearly slaves, bearing tell-tale signs of violence, depredation, and terror. Ghanaian law prohibits slavery, but slaveowners and traffickers told IJM undercover investigators that they had no fear whatsoever of Ghana's antitrafficking police, a force of 150 officers. They have little reason to: the unit does not own a boat and does not patrol Lake Volta. Fortunately, the Government of Ghana is committed to ending this scourge. With training and assistance, the antitrafficking police unit is an excellent candidate for funding and technical assistance from the United States and other donors. Once it begins to rescue kids and apprehend perpetrators, child slavery prevalence will go down—not because Ghana is less economically disadvantaged but because traffickers will respond to increasing prospects of apprehension, conviction and stiff jail terms. Fishing and other enterprises will have to hire—and pay—adult workers.

We've seen and measured the impact of professional law enforcement on the crime of child trafficking elsewhere. In 2007, IJM received a grant from the Bill and Melinda Gates Foundation to begin operations to reduce child sex trafficking in the Philippines second-largest city of Cebu. With that support, IJM initiated collaboration with the Philippines National Police in the country's second-largest city, Cebu, to rescue minor girls from sexual exploitation and apprehend perpetrators. IJM contracted with an independent criminal data collection firm to execute a baseline prevalence of commercial exploitation of minors in Cebu's substantial sex industry. Over the next 3 years, IJM and its PNP partners investigated hundreds of establishments, rescued over 225 victims of trafficking, and apprehended 77 suspected perpetrators. Because trafficking is a nonbail offense under Philippines law, those suspects remained in jail, many of their businesses shuttered. The independent investigators conducted a midterm study and a final study at the end of the 4-year period. They found that the availability of minor girls had plummeted by 79 percent in Cebu.

International Justice Mission has also seen dramatic reduction in the prevalence of child prostitution elsewhere in Southeast Asia as a consequence of professional policing. In Cambodia, very young, prepubescent children were commonly available for sexual exploitation in the early 2000's. A Cambodian Government study at the time estimated that 30 percent of those in prostitution were minor children. A decade later, professional policing by a well-trained and well-led antitrafficking unit had transformed the sex industry in Cambodia. A prevalence study by IJM in late 2012 revealed no children under 15 being sold for sex and very few minors age 15–17 in commercial sex venues.

Cambodia's transformation with regard to commercial sexual exploitation of children is noteworthy because broader human rights standards did not improve. Cambodia's Government was not comprehensively transformed, and it is still a poor country. Change occurred because the government made a conscious political decision to enforce its own laws against child prostitution and proceeded to equip and empower the police antitrafficking unit to do its job. Over 100 perpetrators of child trafficking were convicted and jailed. And Cambodia's criminal class responded with alacrity: they got out of the business of selling children.

IJM's experience working with local law enforcement has shown us that police can improve quite dramatically and are equal to the task of changing the calculations of those profiting from the sale of others. As we've seen in Southeast Asia, it is not necessary for police to apprehend every brothel owner, madam, pimp, or trafficker. A relatively small number of arrests, prosecutions, and convictions have a disproportionate impact on criminals who buy, sell, and exploit children.

The United States has led in the worldwide fight against slavery, and is fortunate to have some excellent tools with which to do it. The Trafficking Victims Protection Act of 2000 and the establishment of the State Department Office to Monitor and Combat Trafficking in Persons have helped make the issue of slavery a top U.S. foreign policy concern. The annual Trafficking in Persons Report has been the catalyst for positive changes by governments on every continent, as has the leadership of many very fine American diplomats around the world.

We are grateful for Congress authorizing and funding an antitrafficking innovation: Child Protection Compacts. We have seen what is possible in our own work when we partnered with local law enforcement in a collaborative casework model, and stayed in the fight with them. The Child Protection Compacts reflects this approach, and offers an opportunity to see real change in the prevalence of child trafficking in selected focus countries.

But even with the substantial diplomatic and financial resources the United States has offered over the past 15 years, the global scourge of slavery requires a global response. IJM is very encouraged by discussions between the Senate, the executive branch, and representatives of the private sector about the creation of a new funding mechanism that would bring new resources to the fight. We look forward to working with you on this historic initiative.

The CHAIRMAN. Thank you.
Shawna.

STATEMENT OF SHAWNA BADER–BLAU, EXECUTIVE DIRECTOR, SOLIDARITY CENTER, WASHINGTON, DC

Ms. BADER-BLAU. Thank you very much, Chairman Corker, and Ranking Member Menendez, and members of the Senate Foreign Relations Committee. And I join Gary in applauding this initiative. It is great to see so many people here today attending this hearing and such a well-attended committee. So thank you for your focus on this issue today.

I will focus my testimony on the aspect of modern slavery that is, in fact, most prevalent, and that is forced labor. The vast majority of the almost 21 million people in forced labor are exploited in the private economy. Trafficking for labor exploitation accounts for 70 percent of trafficked people. Today instead of shackles and chains, people are now likely to be enslaved through threats, debt, and other forms of economic coercion.

The face of modern slavery can be seen in the annual cotton harvest in Uzbekistan, where the government compels teachers and children to pick cotton instead of work or study; in homes in countries as diverse as Lebanon and Singapore where women are enslaved as domestic workers; on construction sites in Saudi Arabia where low-wage migrant construction workers from Nepal and India are trapped in a cycle of debt bondage; and in Cambodia where young women garment workers are locked in factories forced to work until they drop from exhaustion and fear.

Understanding this link between worker rights violations and forced labor is key to eradicating this horrific human rights abuse globally. We see this problem as having four core root causes not currently being adequately addressed that I will lay out. They start with unsafe migration practices. Unsafe migration processes and the lack of labor law and other legal protections for migrant workers make them particularly vulnerable to forced labor.

While stationed in Doha, Qatar, for the Solidarity Center a few years back, I met a young man from Nepal who told me he paid a recruiter $6,000 to get a job there. He was promised a $400 a month salary, and he received only $250, a portion of which was docked for food and accommodation. Deceived by the recruiter in Nepal, he was now tied to his exploitive, abusive employer by the Kafala system in Qatar, and his visa remained with him, and he was not able to leave that employer.

We must create an enabling environment for safe migration as a core way to reduce forced labor globally. This means in part finally getting serious about labor recruiters. Too many manipulate and deceive workers for profit. We need to ban recruitment fees, a primary source of debt bondage and forced labor, promoting universally respected rights for migrant workers so they can speak up and speak out when they see abuse without fear of retaliation. And we need to reform temporary work visa programs so migrants can leave abusive employers instead of staying stuck in forced labor.

And I agree with Gary. It is time to end impunity for labor traffickers. Forced labor is pervasive around the world because employers who engage in modern slavery face few consequences, neither criminal nor economic. Prosecutions for forced labor globally are ridiculously low.

Governments' failure to hold employers criminally accountable for forced labor means that they traffic workers with impunity.

But we also need to make forced labor untenable for governments to allow, and for companies to get away with, including down their supply chain. Like corporations, governments also face few economic penalties or consequences for forced labor. Economic pressure and consequences are effective prevention tools and can involve carrots and sticks. For example, many countries with serious labor trafficking problems continue to receive trade preferences from the United States. And for Mexico, Brunei, Malaysia, and Vietnam, all parties to the Trans-Pacific Partnership, TPP, negotiations, we have a moment now. Lawmakers, in the context of TPP, can work with the administration to make forced labor and modern slavery an issue on the table and negotiate improvements in laws and practices before any new trade agreement goes into force. Indeed, corporations often argue that it is too difficult or too expensive to monitor their entire supply chains, and they need help figuring this out. Well, I agree, but we do need to start asking why. Corporations have innovated to address quality across their supply chains. Why not the eradication of forced labor and slavery, too?

I think we can also promote worker-driven solutions. Workers are also key to eradicating forced labor and trafficking in supply chains. They see abuses or may themselves be exploited on a farm or in a factory. Firsthand reporting of abuses and exploitation by workers, unions, and rights organizations shines a light on abusive practices long before a third party decides to take a look. With rights and protection against retaliation for exposing forced labor conditions, workers can help eradicate modern slavery.

We definitely need a far more robust global response, and a far more robust U.S. Government response. We need significantly greater focus and engagement to address all facets of the problem, especially the root causes of forced labor. Our ultimate goal should be the prevention of this exploitation in the first place, and that is where we should be redoubling our efforts.

Last year, my colleagues in Bangladesh conducted a predeparture training for Bangladeshis traveling to work. Most of them women headed to the gulf as domestic workers. The trainers almost matter of factly told these women, you should know that when you take these jobs, you will more than likely never get paid what you have been promised. You will likely be sexually harassed or worse. And you will have no access to remedy or justice. The class responded back to these trainers, you know, we know that. We are the third generation of families making this trip. We know this might be our fate, but we love our children, and we have no choice but to find a way to provide for them.

Senators, no one trying to support their families or themselves should have to assume exploitation is their fate.

We owe it to mothers like these and millions of other workers like them to fight with them for a world free from extreme labor exploitation that is forced labor. I look forward to discussing this with you further. Thank you.

[The prepared statement of Ms. Bader-Blau follows:]

PREPARED STATEMENT OF SHAWNA BADER-BLAU

Chairman Corker, Ranking Member Menendez, and members of the Senate Foreign Relations Committee, thank you for the opportunity to present the Solidarity Center's perspective on effective policy responses to end modern slavery. We appreciate the committee's continued leadership in combating all forms of human trafficking globally, including trafficking for forced labor.

The Solidarity Center is an international nongovernmental organization (NGO) that promotes and protects worker rights globally, with programs in more than 60 countries. The Solidarity Center is an allied organization of the AFL–CIO and a member of the Alliance to End Slavery and Trafficking (ATEST). Building upon more than 20 years of experience in the areas of child labor, migrant worker exploitation and supply chain accountability, the Solidarity Center raises awareness about the prevalence and underlying causes of forced labor and other forms of trafficking for labor exploitation, and implements programs with partners from myriad sectors to combat the problem. These programs include initiatives that address each of the four ''Ps'' that have become part of the antitrafficking toolkit: prevention, protection of victims, prosecution (or as we prefer to describe it, ''rule of law'') and partnerships. The Solidarity Center has the unique ability to work across borders, in both countries of origin and destination for trafficked workers, as we have long-term, on-the-ground relationships with local partners. Our antihuman trafficking programs span the globe from Africa (Kenya, Sierra Leone), the Americas (Dominican Republic, Mexico), Asia (India, Indonesia, Malaysia, Nepal, Pakistan, the Philippines, Sri Lanka, Thailand), Europe (Moldova) and the Middle East (Jordan, Kuwait, Qatar).

Because I know the leadership of this committee has the desire to take an aggressive approach to ending modern slavery around the world, and because I know that this committee can help us make great strides toward this objective, I will focus my testimony on the aspect of modern slavery that is the most prevalent—and that is forced labor. Most modern slavery today is, in fact, forced labor. That includes government-compelled labor in Uzbekistan during the annual cotton harvest; women enslaved as domestic workers in countries as diverse as Lebanon and Singapore; low-wage migrant construction workers trapped in a cycle of debt bondage in Saudi Arabia; and garment workers locked in factories forced to work for hours on end in Cambodia.

While each country we work in has its own unique context, we have uncovered a common theme. Labor trafficking has, at its core, violations of worker rights and depends on poor labor standards and weak protections to persist. Human trafficking is a worker rights issue because it is linked to various forms of labor exploitation. It is one of the worst forms of worker abuse. Even when the end result of trafficking is sexual exploitation, there are more often than not worker rights issues involved. For example, the Solidarity Center has assisted victims of sex trafficking in Indonesia who were initially recruited by unscrupulous labor brokers who deceived them into leaving their homes by promising them work in the service sector and then forced them into prostitution—often charging them exorbitant sums for the privilege. Indeed, the inspiring trafficking survivor who will speak on the next panel, Ms. Shandra Woworuntu, was by her own account tricked by a labor recruiter promising a real job, only to be forced into prostitution. Around the world, unsafe migration processes, lack of jobs, minimal economic opportunities for women at home and other forms of economic coercion increase the vulnerability of women to sexual exploitation.

Understanding this link between worker rights violations and human trafficking is key to eradicating this horrific human rights abuse globally. To end forced labor, we must address the underlying vulnerability of workers to exploitation, expand and enforce labor laws, and allow workers to organize to monitor their workplaces and improve their wages and working conditions.

In other words, end worker exploitation to end human trafficking.

We increasingly hear the term ''modern slavery'' used to describe the exploitation or compelled service of children, women, and men that results from the myriad forms of coercion and deceptive practices traffickers use. Forced labor, debt bondage, and involuntary servitude are severe forms of labor exploitation that continue today in our modern world, though under a different guise. Instead of shackles and chains, workers are now enslaved through threats, debt, and other forms of economic coercion. And it is a seemingly intractable, growing problem.

More than two decades ago, during a visit to the women's dormitory at Kuwait University, I met a cleaning woman stocking rooms with fresh towels. Originally from India, she asked me what I had seen in downtown Kuwait City: Was it beautiful? She told me she had not been allowed to leave the dormitory courtyard—itself fully encircled by high concrete walls—in 2 years. And even though her husband also lived in Kuwait and drove a taxi in the city, she had not seen him in that same period—men were not permitted on the grounds of the dormitory. I learned that she had paid a lot of money to a recruiter to get the job in Kuwait, and could not leave because of her debt.

Senators, it is beyond outrageous that two decades after she and I met, indentured servitude is still more the norm than the exception for millions of migrant women and men like her working as domestic workers, fishermen, tomato pickers, and garment workers. Today our staff regularly report heartbreaking stories of modern slavery from the more than 60 countries we work in around the world. As we will explore in this hearing, the United States can play an even greater leadership role in helping to combat such egregious abuse around the world.

While governments used to be the primary perpetrators of forced labor, today the vast majority of the almost 21 million people in forced labor globally are exploited in the private economy.[1] Illegal profits made from the use of forced labor worldwide amount to $150 billion per year, exceeding the GDP of many countries.''[2] Moreover, trafficking for labor exploitation is far more prevalent than sex trafficking globally, with 68 percent of the almost 21 million being ''victims of forced labor exploitation, in economic activities such as agriculture, construction, domestic work and manufacturing.''[3]

Modern slavery thrives in a context of private actors and economic coercion. Our response, therefore, must address this context, recognizing human trafficking as more than just sexual exploitation and more than just organized crime. We must move beyond the notion that modern ''slavery is all about bad individuals doing bad things to good people.''[4] We must address what one leading global expert on the international law of human trafficking,[5] calls the ''underlying structures that perpetuate and reward exploitation, including a global economy that relies heavily on exploitation of poor people's labor to maintain growth and a global migration system that entrenches vulnerability and contributes directly to trafficking.''[6] We must exert economic pressure as a response and recognize the protection of worker rights as key to trafficking prevention. We must also reject policies and practices that institutionalize harmful economic and business models that increase workers' vulnerability to human trafficking. We cannot eliminate modern slavery without fundamentally changing how labor migration is managed around the world, how companies do business and how governments monitor and enforce human and labor rights.

It is within this context that I present our recommendations for the most effective policy responses to address gaps in U.S. and global efforts to end human trafficking for labor exploitation.

1. REFORM UNSAFE MIGRATION PRACTICES

Unsafe migration processes and the lack of labor law and other legal protections for migrant workers[7] make them particularly vulnerable to forced labor. And governments clearly lack political will to do much about it. The potential profits to be made from the global labor migration business—by government officials, employers, employment agencies and labor recruiters—seem to trump initiatives to combat the vulnerability of this at-risk population.

It is common business practice for employers to subcontract hiring and human resources management to labor brokers or employment agencies. All too often, labor recruiters compel workers—who have no other viable opportunities for employment in their home village or country—to pay exorbitant recruitment fees for the privilege of laboring under harsh and often inhumane conditions. Many of these migrant workers—seeking only to work toward a better life for themselves and their families—end up trafficked into forced labor and debt bondage, a situation nearly impossible to escape.

While stationed in Doha, Qatar, for the Solidarity Center a few years back, I met a young man from Nepal who told me he paid a recruiter $6,000 to get a construction job in Qatar. Promised a $400 monthly salary, he was paid only $250, a portion of which was docked for food and accommodation. Due to the kafala system, his visa was tied to his employer and he had no choice but to stay. Despite the proven connection between recruitment fees and vulnerability to forced labor,[8] governments and businesses are institutionalizing these practices through increased temporary migration programs and the under- or non-regulation of labor recruiters. Moreover, many governments around the world are complicit in trafficking by labor recruiters by (at best) failing to regulate them or monitor their practices, or (at worst) accepting bribes to turn a blind eye or actually becoming involved in the recruitment of workers for profit themselves.

From poor Bangladeshi women providing household services in Jordanian homes to Nepali construction workers building soccer stadiums for the World Cup in Qatar, and from Cambodian men on Thai boats working to put fish on American grocery store shelves to Mexican workers processing seafood under H–2B visas along the U.S. Gulf Coast,[9] migrant workers around the world are vulnerable to trafficking through the unregulated and unmonitored practices of labor recruiters, even when they migrate through legal channels, with valid visas.

Antitrafficking activists around the world, and in the United States, point to reform of labor recruitment processes and the regulation of labor recruiters as one of the most important initiatives to prevent human trafficking around the world. To this end, the Solidarity Center is working with a coalition of NGOs, trade unions, academics/researchers, and other migrant rights activists to call for global labor recruitment reform, and a commitment from international labor migration policymakers (like at the Global Forum on Migration and Development), governments and businesses to implement a global "no fees" policy for migrant workers. We need a global effort to permanently ban recruitment fees.

We are seeing progress, including the Federal Acquisition Regulations on Ending Trafficking in Persons (for federal contracts) released just last week; the International Labor Organization (ILO) Protocol and Recommendation on Forced Labor adopted after tripartite negotiations in June 2014; and California's law, SB 477, which requires foreign labor contractors to register with the Labor Commissioner.[10] The notion that migrant workers should not have to pay recruitment fees to find a job is increasingly accepted in policy circles. Even a few multinational corporations have adopted "no fees to workers" policies.

Congress can continue to play an important leadership role in ending forced labor by passing a comprehensive law to regulate foreign labor recruiters who hire workers through U.S. nonimmigrant visa programs, such as H1, H2 and J1. The Senate's passage of Subtitle F: Prevention of Trafficking in Persons and Abuses Involving Workers Recruited Abroad and similar provisions in Subtitle I as part of S. 744 (Immigration Reform) in 2013 is a significant step forward in addressing this issue. In the House of Representatives, H.R. 3344, introduced last year by House Committee on Foreign Affairs Chairman, Ed Royce, is modeled after Subtitle F and has bipartisan support, with over 70 cosponsors. Unfortunately, a few large sponsoring companies are opposing these bills, sacrificing poor workers for the bottom line. Still Congress has a real opportunity to enact legislation that could end fraud in our nonimmigrant visa programs and prevent trafficking in the labor recruitment system. Not only will such a law help protect migrant workers in the United States, but it also will serve as a powerful model for other countries, and may influence international labor migration policy.

2. END IMPUNITY FOR LABOR TRAFFICKERS

Systematic abuse of migrant workers, rising to the level of forced labor and human trafficking, goes virtually unpunished throughout world. The State Department's 2014 Trafficking in Persons Report provides numerous examples of governments' reluctance to hold employers accountable for trafficking in their workplaces. And the Los Angeles Times,[11] in a December 2014 series on working conditions at Mexican farms that ship produce to U.S. supermarkets, found that one of Mexico's largest growers routinely withheld wages from workers, housed them in rat-infested facilities and allowed bosses to beat workers who tried to escape. Two company employees were even charged with human trafficking. The government levied fines against that farm, Bioparques de Occidente, but after the uproar subsided, those fines seem to have melted away. The men accused of trafficking have not been tried nor can the charges against them be confirmed.

Immigration officials around the world regularly categorize migrant workers who are labor trafficking victims as undocumented or "out of status" workers and deport them. Police and labor inspectors often view involuntary servitude, debt bondage, or forced labor in sectors such as agriculture, domestic work, construction, manual labor and manufacturing as "mere worker rights violations" that do not require their intervention.

Even in the rare cases when labor trafficking is identified and charges brought, the labor recruiter is blamed and not the employer who also perpetrates the exploitation. This lack of political will translates into pathetically few cases of human trafficking for forced labor or other forms of severe labor exploitation being prosecuted globally. According to the 2014 Trafficking in Persons Report, there were only 9,460 prosecutions and 5,776 convictions for trafficking globally in 2013; of these, only 1,199 cases of forced labor were prosecuted. Governments' failure to hold employers accountable criminally for forced labor means that employers can exploit workers with impunity, and an important trafficking prevention tool goes unutilized.

Solidarity Center partners face this lack of political will to prosecute forced labor on a daily basis in their work. For example, our partner in Thailand, the Human Rights and Development Foundation (HRDF), is currently pursing cases on behalf of four Burmese migrant workers who were trafficked onto fishing boats after paying exorbitant recruitment fees to brokers. Two of the workers tried to commit suicide by jumping off of the ship. Though these cases have been going on for more than a year and HRDF has collected significant evidence, Thai police have yet to charge any broker, boat captain, or boat owner for the abuses.

When cases are prosecuted, they often result in small fines and no jail time for the perpetrators—barely a deterrent for exploitative employers reaping vast profit from the misery of others. Other cases may get put on hold for years while perpetrators are out on bail. Moreover, whistleblowers, in the form of trade union or NGO activists, journalists and migrant workers, often face retaliation for raising issues of forced labor and corruption linked to human trafficking.[12]

While public awareness campaigns and education for at-risk groups are important tools for prevention, one of the key ways to prevent forced labor is to create an enabling environment through the rule of law that promotes transparency and accountability. Increasing prosecutions and convictions, and imposing harsh penalties (including significant jail time and economic restitution) may be an even more effective prevention tool. Workers must have easily accessible avenues to report violations and attain justice, without fear of retaliation—and government officials must be trained and encouraged to respond quickly and effectively.[13]

The Solidarity Center sees the low levels of forced labor prosecutions, lack of political will and impunity as evidence of many governments' dismissal of forced labor as a serious issue. Labor migration is seen as a profitmaking mechanism, for employers, owners of recruitment agencies and government officials, and human trafficking as just an unfortunate consequence.

3. MONITOR AND ENFORCE LAWS REGULATING FORCED LABOR IN SUPPLY CHAINS

Given our globalized economy, the link between worker exploitation and human trafficking in the context of forced labor perpetrated by private actors through economic coercion means that products made with forced labor are ending up on our store shelves. And, governments and businesses are doing little to ensure that supply chains are untainted by forced labor and human trafficking.

In general, it is difficult to quantify the extent of forced labor in global supply chains. But as those supply chains reach down to more and more suppliers, the chances that trafficked people are in the labor force increase. For example:

- When buyers and multinational corporations demand cheap or unrealistic pricing structures from suppliers, severe labor abuses, including forced labor, often result in their supply chains.[14]
- Similarly, when employers contract out or hire unregulated subcontracted suppliers, or rely on labor recruiters and employment agencies, they should not be surprised to find that they have trafficking victims in their production lines.
- When employers refuse to enforce or claim that it is too difficult to monitor adherence to core labor standards in their supply chains, the probability that they will find forced labor, debt bondage, and other severe forms of labor exploitation increases.

The U.S. Government has two important resources at its disposable to monitor industries in countries with a high prevalence of forced labor and vulnerability to other forms of modern slavery. The annual Department of State's (DOS) ''Trafficking in Persons Report'' and the Department of Labor's (DOL) ''List of Goods Produced with Child Labor or Forced Labor Report'' are excellent resources to help identify vulnerable economic sectors for forced labor. Products identified on the DOL's list from countries identified by DOS as having significant labor trafficking problems, however, continue to enter the United States, meaning that in all likelihood the U.S. Government is allowing imports of products made with forced labor.

In 2008, the Solidarity Center released a report as part of its Degradation of Work series titled, ''The True Cost of Shrimp: How Shrimp Industry Workers in Bangladesh and Thailand Pay the Price for Affordable Shrimp.'' Thailand is one of the main exporters of shrimp to the United States. The report uncovered major human rights abuses in the industry: unpaid wages, unsafe and unhealthy workplaces, child labor, forced labor, physical intimidation, violence and sexual abuse. Seven years later, little progress has been made to clean up the industry, as reports continue to surface about human trafficking of migrant workers in the fishing and sea-food-processing sector in Thailand.[15] ''The Guardian'' found that such forced labor plays an integral part in the production of shrimp sold in leading supermarkets around the world, including in the United States, in stores such as Walmart and Costco.[16]

And despite U.S. laws that prohibit the importation of goods made with forced or child labor, Thai shrimp continues to be found at major U.S. retailers and in consumers' freezers. Mexican chilies, more easily plucked by children's hands from 3-foot plants,[17] are processed into salsa for U.S. dinners. Similar concerns may be raised about products such as ready-made garments from Haiti and Jordan, or electronics from Malaysia.

The U.S. Government must do more to ensure that multinational corporations are held accountable for their practices abroad. And we must increase government scrutiny of imports to ensure goods made by forced labor are not allowed into the U.S. marketplace. This type of economic consequence will be a catalyst for change.

The 1930 Tariff Act prohibits the importation of goods into the United States made with forced or child labor. This law, however, is rarely enforced as the ''consumptive demand exception'' weakens it. As required by the 2005 Trafficking Victims Prevention Reauthorization Act (TVPRA), the U.S. Department of Labor ''maintains a list of goods and their source countries which it has reason to believe are produced by child labor or forced labor in violation of international standards.''[18] Even though many of the goods on the list are produced for export by the identified countries, the list has not been used to enforce the Tariff Act.

Moreover, U.S. Immigration and Customs Enforcement (ICE) must notify foreign governments of its intent to inspect workplaces that export products to the United States. Such notification results in the ''cleansing'' of workplaces to remove any signs of trafficking or forced or child labor. Moreover, U.S. law does not allow evidence collected by unions, the media, or nongovernmental sources to be the basis for restricting the importation of products made by trafficked or forced labor. This must be reformed. The Department of Homeland Security must review and rework the role of ICE in overseas inspections.

Many countries that have been shown to have significant labor trafficking problems continue to receive trade preferences from the U.S. Government. Mexico, Brunei, Malaysia and Vietnam, four countries with significant forced labor problems, are part of the Trans-Pacific Partnership (TPP) negotiations. Lawmakers have a significant opportunity in the context of TPP to call out forced labor and modern slavery in these states and negotiate over improvements in laws and practices before any new trade agreement goes into force. If we really want new tools in the struggle against modern slavery, Congress can urge the administration to use the leverage it has right now to negotiate meaningful changes to laws and practices before the agreement takes effect, not after—and to ensure any final trade deal includes vigorous monitoring and enforcement standards.

Congress should also encourage and support the U.S. Trade Representative (USTR) to suspend Generalized System of Preferences (GSP) and other trade benefits for any country that does not effectively address forced labor. Economic consequences are key to eradicating forced labor. And countries that are habitual abusers of vulnerable workers should face trade sanctions. Moreover, bilateral and multilateral trade agreements should contain labor standards and protections to prevent trafficking, ensuring those standards apply to all workers, including migrants.

4. PROMOTE WORKER-DRIVEN SOLUTIONS

Multinational corporations' codes of conduct—which are voluntary and unenforceable—have failed to protect workers from forced labor in supply chains. Solidarity Center staff see examples of this first hand in garment/textile, agriculture, and seafood processing across four continents. Research shows what does NOT work: private, voluntary corporate social auditing and other traditional "corporate social responsibility" (CSR) approaches have proliferated over the last 20 years but on the whole have failed to adequately address labor exploitation and modern slavery in global supply chains.[19]

Indeed, despite their codes of conduct, corporations often argue that it is too difficult or too expensive for them to map and monitor their entire supply chains. However, in the case of Mexican tomatoes, the Los Angeles Times reporter and a photographer—on a newspaper budget—managed to track gross violations throughout the export agriculture industry, including child labor, and follow supply chains to U.S. grocery stores. In addition, the Times reported the regular presence of buyers inspecting produce, just feet from abused workers.[20] Obviously, whatever corporate social responsibility guidelines those companies have in place carry little weight—and other pressure is required.

Companies can and should do more. Secretary of State John Kerry summed up the situation last week, at the White House Forum on Combating Human Trafficking in Supply Chains:[21] "Governments can lead the way in ensuring that suppliers and contractors are held to the highest standards and adopt the highest standards. Companies can enforce regulations against human trafficking throughout their supply chains, and that includes the production of raw materials, labor brokers, contractors, and subcontractors throughout the final product."

Still, workers are key to eradicating forced labor and trafficking in supply chains. Workers see abuses or may be the exploited on a farm or in a factory. We know that firsthand reporting of abuses and exploitation by workers, unions, and rights organizations shine a light on abusive practices through on-the-ground investigations and worker whistleblowing. It is crucial that the U.S. Government support monitoring and the efforts of workers to report human rights violations in their own workplaces, without fear of retaliation. Ultimately, workers and trade unions must be empowered to monitor supply chains because history shows that abuses in the workplace only end when workers can assert their rights under ILO conventions and national laws are respected. Employers and governments must therefore support and respect the freedom of association for workers.

We should embrace proven worker-driven models of corporate accountability like the Coalition of Immokalee Workers' Fair Food Program, which is an excellent example of how economic consequences can help to eliminate forced labor and other forms of labor trafficking in an industry.[22] Governments should impose trade restrictions, import bans or other penalties on products made with forced labor, and multinational corporations should exert their significant power as buyers to hold suppliers accountable to supply chains free of forced labor.

Finally, freedom from forced labor and slavery are established human rights principles. The United Nations Guiding Principles for Business and Human Rights provide a powerful and inclusive baseline that can be employed in the global fight to end modern slavery.[23]

TOWARD A ROBUST U.S. GOVERNMENT RESPONSE

Addressing the role of private actors in forced labor and modern slavery that is perpetuated through the use of economic coercion requires an integrated approach—promoting worker rights, increasing access to justice, ensuring safe migration and focusing on economic growth that promotes shared prosperity. It is also requires an integrated approach by government.

The U.S. Government has shown true leadership in the global fight against human trafficking, including expanding the understanding that human trafficking is also about labor exploitation. But as we continue to learn about the scope and magnitude of modern slavery, we know that much remains to be done. We need significantly greater resources, and we need approaches that address all facets of the problem, and especially the underlying root causes of human trafficking. While it is crucial to identify and protect victims, prosecute perpetrators, our ultimate goal of course is to prevent the exploitation in the first place.

The U.S. Department of State's Office to Monitor and Combat Trafficking in Persons (J/TIP) plays an absolutely crucial role in pressuring and supporting governments around the world to address modern slavery. The effectiveness of the J/TIP office given its small size is commendable. Importantly, and with bipartisan consensus, it has raised the profile of forced labor and human trafficking within our government and has had unmatched influence on how multilateral institutions, private actors, and governments around the world define and address the scourge of modern slavery. The tier rankings and accompanying diplomacy provide one of the most effective tools the United States government has for promoting accountability to human rights in our entire foreign policy agenda.

As a lifelong activist and passionate defender of human and labor rights, I can tell you how refreshing it is—and how incredibly unusual it is—to see such regular coherence of policy, diplomacy, and program support for work on the ground around the world that comes out of J/TIP. J/TIP receives less than $20 million a year for its grantmaking program. Increased resources for J/TIP could greatly expand its ability to coordinate the U.S. Government response to trafficking, and allow J/TIP to focus more of its attention on prevention efforts globally. And it is absolutely crucial that the new Ambassador for the J/TIP office be committed to addressing both labor and sex trafficking; be able to take on recalcitrant governments; and be a unifying, not polarizing, force in the antitrafficking movement.

And this committee also oversees other agencies in the U.S. Government that are fundamental to combating forced labor around the world. They include the State Department's Bureau of Democracy, Human Rights and Labor (DRL), which promotes human rights, including worker rights, as a way to prevent human trafficking. DRL could do much more to help eradicate modern slavery if it was given the policy direction and resources to mainstream the promotion of the migrant rights agenda further within the Department of State and U.S. embassies. The Department of Labor's Bureau of International Labor Affairs (ILAB), which provides technical assistance to governments on how to implement and enforce core labor standards as a way to prevent forced labor and child labor, is responsible for producing the annual List of Goods Produced with Child Labor or Forced Labor required by the Trafficking Victims Protection Act (TVPA). ILAB engages with businesses and workers to address root causes of forced labor, and has championed the importance of using rigorous data collection and analysis in this struggle. The U.S. Agency for International Development (USAID), through its Counter-Trafficking in Persons (C–TIP) policy and country based programs, is finding ways to integrate antitrafficking initiatives into all of USAID's strategic objectives. Despite the clear connection between economic, social, and democratic development and the prevention of severe forms of labor exploitation, all of these agencies are too understaffed and underresourced to address the scope of the problem.

Finally, we are encouraged that the Senate is discussing ways to spur a bold and more aggressive global approach to ending these enduring horrific human rights abuses that are the focus of the hearing today. A successful new initiative will:

- Prioritize an approach that addresses all forms of trafficking, e.g., sex trafficking and labor trafficking.
- Embrace principles of transparency, accountability, and survivor leadership in interventions; ensuring that trafficking survivors, civil society, and worker organizations have meaningful input and participation.
- Build on the steady progress of current U.S. Government efforts, and not rechannel resources that are currently authorized to combat trafficking domestically and globally, but rather represent an additional investment by the U.S. Government to supplement the meager resources available today in relation to the scale and severity of the crime.
- Support coordination among agencies to ensure a comprehensive, holistic approach to combating human trafficking. This includes working in close cooperation with international agencies, such as the International Labor Organization.
- Be linked to the priorities and recommendations in the annual "TIP Report" and the "List of Goods Report"; and, reports of United Nations agencies, such as the International Labor Organization.

Thank you again for the opportunity to testify and for your continued leadership in combating trafficking for forced labor and other forms of severe labor exploitation around the world. I welcome your questions.

End Notes

[1] "International Labor Organization (ILO) Global Estimate of Forced Labor."

[2] Profits and Poverty: The Economics of Forced Labor, International Labor Organization, 2014.

[3] The ILO estimates that out of the 21 million, 4.5 million (22% total) are victims of forced sexual exploitation. ILO Global Estimate of Forced Labor.

[4] Gallagher, Anne T., The Global Slavery Index—Seduction and Obfuscation, November 28, 2014.

[5] Anne Gallagher was named a "TIP Report Hero" in the 2012 Department of State "Trafficking in Persons Report."

[6] Id.

[7] The term "migrant worker" is the internationally accepted term for a person who migrates for employment, whether temporary, seasonally, or permanently. In the United States, in everyday language, "migrant worker" may refer to a seasonal or temporary worker, and "immigrant worker" refers to someone who migrates for work on a more permanent basis or who has residency rights. I will use the term "migrant worker" in my testimony to refer to all workers who migrate for work, regardless of their status or length of stay in the destination country.

[8] In its Profits and Poverty report, the ILO found "the payment of recruitment fees, even to relatives or friends, leads to a higher probability of ending up in forced labor."

[9] See for example "Summary of Preliminary Audit of U.S. Walmart Suppliers that Employ Guestworkers." National Guestworker Alliance.

[10] SB 477: Requires foreign labor contractors to register with the Labor Commissioner and penalizes intimidation, discrimination, and other violations to prevent the exploitation of foreign workers.

[11] "Desperate Workers on a Mexican Mega-Farm: 'They Treated Us like Slaves'". Los Angeles Times. December 11, 2014.

[12] For example, a U.S. labor rights group, the National Guestworkers Alliance, found evidence that Mexican workers in one Louisiana plant were coerced by their employer into working in dangerous conditions against their will by threatening to harm their families, specifically their children, in Mexico. The workers understood this treat to be real as the owner bragged about knowing "bad people" who would do his bidding.

[13] Congress and other governments must pass national whistleblower protection laws (such as the "Protect Our Workers from Exploitation and Retaliation," or POWER Act) regarding trafficked and vulnerable migrant workers. Such legislation would serve as a model for other governments globally. Also, companies should ensure that there are worker protections in company policy all along the supply chain, and advocate to governments for such protections.

[14] The pricing structure as a cause of human trafficking cannot be overemphasized, as this is an underlying factor that employers, business, corporations, and consumers can all address. As described in the Solidarity Center's report, The True Cost of Shrimp: "As a commodity, the price of shrimp fluctuates according to supply and demand, and price pressure is significant all along the supply chain. Retailers, sensitive to the risk involved with importing fresh food, press import companies for faster distribution, acceptable quality and the lowest prices. Importers, aware that market fluctuations can affect prices, leverage their bulk purchasing power to demand speedy delivery from producers. Trapped between producers and importers are labor-intensive shrimp factories. Often, the factories' response to price pressure is to squeeze wages, neglect workplace health and safety regulations, and cut other corners that leave shrimp workers bearing the social cost of affordable shrimp." The True Cost of Shrimp, Solidarity Center, 2008, p. 11.

[15] See for example: "Trafficked into Slavery on Thai Trawlers to Catch Food for Prawns," The Guardian, June 10, 2014.

[16] See "Revealed: Asian Slave Labor Producing Prawns for Supermarkets in U.S., U.K.," The Guardian, June 10, 2014. See also "Thailand's Seafood Industry: A Case of State-Sanctioned Slavery?" The Guardian, June 10, 2014.

[17] "In Mexico's Fields, Children Toil to Harvest Crops that Make it to American Tables." Los Angeles Times. December 14, 2014.

[18] http://www.dol.gov/ilab/reports/child-labor/list-of-goods/.

[19] See "Responsibility Outsourced: Social Audits, Workplace Certification and Twenty Years of Failure to Protect Worker Rights" AFL–CIO April 2013.

[20] "Desperate Workers on a Mexican Mega-Farm . . . " Los Angeles Times.

[21] Remarks at the White House Forum on Combating Human Trafficking in Supply Chains. U.S. Department of State. January 29, 2015.

[22] http://ciw-online.org/slavery/ and http://ciw-online.org/fair-food-program/.

[23] The U.N. Guiding Principles were adopted unanimously by the U.N. Human Rights Council in 2011. They recognize that when it comes to human rights, the State has the duty to protect, Corporations have the responsibility to respect these rights, and Victims have the right to access remedies when violated and provide implementation guidance to states and corporations.

The CHAIRMAN. Well, thank you both. Great testimony and we really appreciate your efforts in being here and your efforts regarding this issue.

I have come to believe that through Congress, we can create and lead a vision to end modern day slavery. I really believe that. And we have had conversations with both the private sector and public sector—some partners around the world. I really believe that, undoubtedly, with the United States behind it, we can lead, we can solve this, and we can bring others to the table.

One of the things that I have learned is that many organizations are adopting best practices, okay? And, Gary, if I could, my staff has prepared a number of questions, but I was able to go to the Philippines and see your work there. And I would just say to the audience and the people here that seeing the 22 young women that we saw that day, you would have to be not a human being to sit through that with dry eyes.

I would just like, with my time, if you could just walk through how you go into a jurisdiction and build from the ground up the type of effort that you just talked about so that others might hear.

Mr. HAUGEN. Thank you, Mr. Chairman. Well, it begins by where all the best information comes, and that is by actually walking alongside the victims of slavery. If you do not actually get close to them and understand their experience, you just will never be able to serve them in a way that ends slavery. But it also means having to get to know the experience of the perpetrators, the people who do this.

What will make them afraid to try to enslave another person? So what we do is we go and we begin to work cases. We work with local partners there on the ground. We raise up a local national team of investigators and lawyers and social workers, and they proactively go find where are the victims of slavery. Then we take those cases to the actual authorities, and we do something we call collaborative case work. We actually begin to work cases with the authorities.

And what you find out is what is broken in law enforcement that could be fixed in order to make sure that the law is enforced because it is thriving because it is not. So, it requires working these cases through the system and finding where is it broken. And in that process you make a diagnosis that is not just about blaming. It is about improving a capacity.

And so, what we have now seen is that you can improve the police capacity, the prosecution, the courts, and, critically, the survivor care services in a way that actually brings hope. We have seen in the Philippines, for instance, measurable decreases of sex trafficking of kids by about 80 percent over about only a 4-year period of time because enforcement kicked in. We walked alongside them with collaborative case work, began to transform the system, and then did what we are doing now, which is making sure that the community owns and imbeds that victory so that it goes on without IJM's engagement.

What has happened in the Philippines, the success in the second-largest city so inspired the government to then continue this model in Manila, the largest city, and Pampanga, another city that had the largest sex trafficking of kids. And so, what you do is you restore hope to the system, and law enforcement can actually do its job.

We did not have to substantially reduce poverty in the Philippines over those 4 years. Other programs were getting after that, and that is important in reducing their vulnerability. But we did not have to wait for that to happen to see a nearly 80 percent reduction in the victimization of kids in the commercial sex trade. Is that helpful, Mr. Chairman?

The CHAIRMAN. So, the question is, I mean, as we begin to look at doing something, mobilizing on a global scale, is what you have done there, in your opinion, something that can be replicated around the world where slavery is just a part of the culture there?

Mr. HAUGEN. We have no doubt about that. Some places will be harder than others. We are working in South Asia, Southeast Asia, Africa, Latin America, really different contexts. But one thing is certainly true. It seems like a culturally acceptable practice as long as no one gets in trouble for it. But when people start to get marched off to jail for it, everyone starts to realize, oh, yes, this is against the law. The law can actually be enforced, and I do not want to be in this business anymore.

That is a transferrable concept. We have seen it now replicated due to some private financial support in South Asia that has allowed us to replicate to now dozens of other organizations who can do the exact same thing.

The CHAIRMAN. You know, you compared this to malaria. We have had some of the same results in PEPFAR because we have continued to focus on treatment, although there is always a push, as you mentioned earlier, to sort of move out into other areas. But if you focus on treatment, then you have the kind of results, and we have been able to do that. This committee has been able to make sure that the focus is on treatment.

One of the things that I think people would be concerned about is how do you know you are achieving the results that are laid out with an issue like this? Could you talk to us a little bit about how you set the base and how we can actually measure the results in a way that if we were to lead an effort like this, we would know that we were actually achieving results?

Mr. HAUGEN. This is absolutely critical, Senator, as you think about stewarding the taxpayer's money, of making an investment in the fighting against slavery. Could you actually measure that it is working? This has never been done before until the last decade where we now can go into communities and do prevalence studies. We can measure how much sex trafficking, forced labor is actually taking place by infiltrating the criminal networks who are operating and get a baseline. Then you can carry out your intervention and measure at a halfway point, and then at the end, whether or not there has actually been two things: one, an increase in the performance of the criminal justice system in enforcement, and then a correlated decrease in the prevalence of the slavery.

I do not think we should be going forward with significant investments in fighting slavery unless there is measurement about whether or not those efforts are succeeding. Are they suceeding in trying hard? No. In lots of activity? No. In training at fun days at the Sheraton? No. But did it actually measurably reduce the amount of slavery over time? That is now possible, and that is the huge development that now gives us a moment in history to get rid of slavery.

The CHAIRMAN. And in closing, Shawna, in listening to that, I know you have had a tremendous amount of experience in supply chains and efforts in that regard. Do you think we are at a point in time where we can measure success and that these types of best practices can be multiplied in other places around the world?

Ms. BADER-BLAU. I absolutely do, and I do agree that the United States has a very important role to play here. In fact, the agencies of the U.S. Government and departments of the U.S. Government that are focused on forced labor and trafficking, woefully underfunded as they are, have been making some good innovations in these efforts. The Department of Labor's International Labor Affairs Bureau, for example, has focused more on data collection, and monitoring, and best practices, and replication.

I would say that the TIP office of the State Department, I think it is, in fact, and I can say this having looked across our foreign assistance framework. Our work out of the TIP office, as underfunded and small of an effort as it is compared to what we need in the world, is one of the places where we have a very coherent policy and programmatic orientation where together policies and programs and directed in the service of diplomacy fighting this scourge globally. And if we could bring more resources to that fight, I think that office could do a lot more as well.

The State Department, the Bureau of Democracy, Human Rights, and Labor, has a role to play on root causes and identifying root causes around the global migration problem.

Some of the issues I discussed around recruitment fees and the extreme labor exploitation and forced labor conditions of domestic workers, for example, that we see in the gulf. Our diplomacy should be much more robust and aggressive on tackling the root causes of this very difficult form of modern slavery that is hard to eradicate, but is the real truth of the lives of domestic workers in dozens of countries around the world.

So, there are programs that work and can be replicated. And I would really enjoy working with the committee to flesh some of those out. I can name just one really quickly. In Florida, you will know of the program of the Coalition of Immokalee Workers, Fair Food Program, working with several international U.S.-based companies has figured out a way to eradicate forced labor in tomatoes in Florida through a program jointly with big buyers. And that has been a really successful, highly regarded program. It is actually a worker-driven program. It is called the Fair Food Program there in Immokalee, FL.

We also had a great experience in Liberia on the Bridgestone Plantation where for decades we had a very bad problem with child labor there. And with the democratic opening at the end of the civil war in Liberia and the emergence of civil society in the country, an organization formed there, the Firestone Agricultural Workers Union of Liberia. They were able to work with the company to lower quotas that were causing all these children to have to work with their families in order to meet the quotas, and they lowered these quotas through bargaining. Together they lowered the quotas that were demanded of each worker, so husbands did not have to bring their children and wives to help them meet these quotas. And in so doing, they created a new stream of funding to pay for schools on that planation, and today child labor has been eradicated on that plantation. It is really a success story that we could invest in and a model we could work on globally.

The CHAIRMAN. Thank you for that full answer, and I am sorry I went over just a little bit. As we turn to our distinguished ranking member—thank you both again—Senator Menendez.

Senator MENENDEZ. Thank you, Mr. Chairman. Mr. Chairman, you get to go over as long as you want as far as I am concerned. In any event, thank you both for your testimony and, more importantly, for your work.

I want to start with you, Mr. Haugen. Basically, I heard your overarching theme is that we have to end impunity if we want to end slavery at the end of the day, modern day slavery. And so, that to me means in addition to the infrastructure that your ministry has built and working on creating the access to those who are the victims of slavery, bringing their stories and information to light, it means governments have to have a willingness to fight because impunity ultimately prevails if governments are not willing ultimately to prosecute.

So I heard you in response to the chairman talk about how some of the work that you have done has helped governments incline, but have you found governments that are not inclined to put a priority to the question of ending impunity in modern slavery? And if so, how do we break through with those governments?

Mr. HAUGEN. Sure. To be clear, I think in every setting where we have started, the government was disinclined to invest in this effort, so we are always up against the lack of political will. Three things have been super powerful. One is rallying the local community to demand that their local government do a better job, and there are heroes, local organizations, leaders that can be rallied to that, and we have seen that shift. And what you do is you end up giving them a lot of the evidence and clarity about the nature of the problem.

Secondly, international influence matters tremendously. So in countries like the Philippines and Cambodia, it mattered tremendously that this was a priority of U.S. diplomatic interaction. We saw the situation change from not being an interest at all to the local government, to becoming a huge interest.

The third thing that is really quite interesting now is that the private sector has a powerful role to play because there are very, very large international corporations that carry reputation exposure because they have forced labor in their supply chains. And so, now they are getting a lot of proper pressure, and there are things they can do to take care of it themselves. But what they also can do is to begin to turn their attention to those local governments and say, hey, we are getting all this exposure because you do not enforce these laws at all. To begin to direct that kind of influence will matter.

The fourth thing that matters tremendously is demonstrating what is possible. A lot of what looks like a lack of political will is despair. They do not think it is possible to get the police to actually enforce the laws without corruption and with excellence. We have seen that once you put together a unit that can do that and demonstrate it is possible, people get a vision for it, and things move very fast.

Senator MENENDEZ. And when you were talking about creating community support, I would assume those are individuals who are not the victims of trafficking, but others in the community who bore the slavery and trafficking that is taking place, and try to create a change in their government. Is that right?

Mr. HAUGEN. Absolutely, local organizations.

Senator MENENDEZ. And let me ask you this. What can we do from your experience, what can governments, and the private sector, and the public sector do to increase protections for potential trafficking victims during conflicts, which increasingly seems to be one of our challenges?

Mr. HAUGEN. Yes, that is, I think, the largest challenge for us is trying to address trafficking in sectors where there is no rule of law. It is a failed state. It is a conflict zone. One of the things that absolutely we can begin to do much better is what Shawna alluded to is make sure that those who are fleeing those conflicts and are refugees, displaced people, to make sure that they are just not in floating circles of sort of lawless chaos, that there are ways to make sure that they are reasonably well protected, and so that we look to see whether or not there is actually law enforcement that is protecting those populations and regulation of the treatment of those that are fleeing those zones.

I am not going to tell you that it is going to be possible to effectively enforce these antislavery laws in places where there is an ongoing war. But we can reduce the vulnerability of those who are displaced by it, and we can go to the places where most of the slaves are, which are not conflict zones. They are reasonably peaceful, stable countries where simply they do not actually enforce the laws against slavery. That is where the tens of millions are.

Senator MENENDEZ. Ms. Bader-Blau, I am interested. You mentioned Qatar as one of your examples. In January, I sent a letter to the Secretary of State with our concerns about the realities of forced labor and foreign labor during Qatar's infrastructure projects in advance of the 2022 World Cup. And while we applaud Qatar for winning the site of the World Cup, we also know that in this lead-up to the dramatic infrastructure work that needs to take place, there are real challenges to some of the workers who are falling in the same type of slavery that you acknowledge. So I will look forward to seeing the Secretary's response to that.

So, you gave some pretty powerful examples of what workers themselves can do as it relates to trying to end human trafficking and slavery, particularly in the labor context. What more can governments do to end forced labor in the supply chain, and what more can the private sector do? Mr. Haugen said that there is a powerful incentive for the private sector to get it right because they do not want to have their brand tarnished. In a different context, I have been pursuing this with workers in Bangladesh. The question I want to know from you from your perspective, what can the governments do to create a more powerful action against the impunity, and also what can corporations do.

Ms. BADER-BLAU. Thank you, and I think those are the key questions really. You know, if I could start with government and if I could start with our own government, you know, looking at—you started with the example of Qatar. In fact, the entire gulf has a problem with extreme forced labor, Saudi Arabia being a major challenge as well as the United Arab Emirates and Kuwait. The whole gulf has this problem.

When I spent time in the gulf, what I found is when you talk to migrant workers, they say that their governments where they come from do not do anything to help them. And when you talk to the governments privately, what they tell you is, well, you know, if we tell Saudi Arabia or Qatar that we demand a minimum wage of $350 a month for our construction workers, they will just say we will not take you, we will take Burmese workers instead. And so, there is a power dynamic between the wealthy countries that are importing labor and the home countries that view migration as an important development tool for themselves. It is a commodification really of the poorest people on the planet through this system.

And I think the United States could actually fill a major gap here working with other major countries to get the home and host countries together that are playing this very, very bad race to the bottom game with the lives of very, very poor people around the world, and say, look, stop this race to the bottom. The Burmese construction workers are cheaper than the Indians, are cheaper than the Nepalese. Have a convening of the home country countries and talk about how that leads to forced labor and trafficking.

I think we also really need to address this question of recruitment fees, and the United States can do so much more on this question. I cannot tell you how many people I have met in my experience who say the reason I have to stay in the despicable working conditions I am, and the people we do not see that I could not even meet because they are trapped in a home and are not allowed out, is because they owe tens of thousands of dollars in some cases to recruiters.

This recruitment agency around the world, these agencies need to be better regulated, and we need to play a bigger role in that. They operate often under the radar in an illegal manner. They are not regulated by their states. They often operate with mafia-like tendencies in many countries and extort money from very desperate people. Without any focus on any regulation on the recruitment industry, the chance that we are going to end this part of slavery that is debt bondage and forced labor is very, very low. So I think we could play a very serious leadership role there.

In terms of corporations, I think corporations are really the key since most forced labor today is in the private economy around the world, and I think the question of supply chains is a tough one. There is endless subcontracting out that happens to keep prices down. Well, the real question is, at what point do we say to ourselves that it is time for corporations to say, yes, I agree, I would like to eradicate forced labor in my supply chain? I am going to make this a priority, and I am going to hold myself accountable to this. And so, therefore, I am going to make the entire chain transparent. I will let everyone know who our subcontractors are. And I will, as a CEO, I will guarantee that we are going to work directly with each subcontractor down the chain to make sure that they prove there is no forced labor and no slavery there.

We have been able to achieve amazing innovations in the private sector through incredibly good focus on quality control through supply chains. I know that we can do this to end forced labor as well, and I think this committee could play a real role in that regard. I think there are a lot of good examples there to be had.

Senator MENENDEZ. Thank you. Thank you, Mr. Chairman.

The CHAIRMAN. Thank you. Thank you, Senator.

Senator Risch.

Senator RISCH. Thank you very much, and thank you for your testimony. One thing that you did not pay much attention to, something that struck me in the years I have been on this committee and on the Intelligence Committee, is a condition around the world that most Americans really are unaware of, and probably would be surprised that in the United States and only a handful of other countries, bribery is not acceptable.

In listening to witnesses from all over the world talking about the issues that they have, particularly when it comes to nonenforcement of laws, bribery seems to be ubiquitous around the world. And obviously the less money there is, the more powerful money becomes. A person who wants to stay in power, be it through votes or whatever else, will ignore the rule of law in order to garner votes. And it surprises me how ubiquitous it is, how acceptable it is, how in parts of the world it has quasi-legal status, even legal status in some parts of the world.

So, what do you do when you run into this? First of all, is this an area of your concern, and secondly, what do you when you run into that where, okay, you have found the problem, you have identified who the people are, who the actors are. You have got a law that is on the books. And, like you said, there is reluctance on the government's part, and probably at least on occasion that it is a result of bribery. What do you do in that kind of a—first of all, how common is this, and then, secondly, what do you do with it? Mr. Haugen first.

Mr. HAUGEN. Just to affirm, Senator, it is massively common. Every context we have gone into we have seen overwhelming police corruption, corruption of the criminal justice system, which gets paid not to enforce the law. And this can seem like a completely overwhelming situation until you adopt the perspective of the enslaver or the trafficker, which is from their corruption: What do they need? A reduced probability that they will not get in trouble? No. They need certainty that they will not get in trouble, and so they need all the bribes they need to make sure that they are safe.

What happens, however, when you introduce a vetted, trained, specialized unit that is actually enforcing the law—it is going around a rogue force and enforcing the law—and it completely disrupts the corruption network because now I am paying money, but it is not guaranteeing me safety. And so, we have seen this incredibly powerful effort, or effect really, of vetted units that can disrupt these corruption networks so you do not have to actually clean up all the corruption before you get results. You can establish some vetted, trained units that are enforcing the law, and it makes that perpetrator get out of the business because he cannot buy certainty anymore.

We have also found what we call the 15/70/15 rule in law enforcement. Fifteen percent of police show up to try to steal and hurt people every day, 15 percent show up trying to do the right thing, and the 70 percent in the middle, they are just waiting to see who is going to prevail. And when the corrupt ones are prevailing, they are right there with the corrupt officers, and it looks like that system is 85 percent corrupt.

But when the corrupt officers start going to jail, they start failing to get the jobs, and the promotions and the success and rewards go to those who are actually succeeding, that 70 in the middle who wants to keep their jobs, they just scoot themselves right over. And that starts to very quickly look like a police department that is pretty much 85 percent functioning. This transformation we have seen with our own eyes in countries across cultures, and it is very encouraging.

Senator RISCH. That is assuming, of course, they cannot get to the people at the top that are hiring these units that will go out there.

Mr. HAUGEN. Yes, sir, but that has been surprising that we have seen that in most contexts it does not go all the way to the top.

Senator RISCH. It operates at the lower levels.

Mr. HAUGEN. Yes, sir. They will not want to necessarily proactively address the patronage of people that they are protecting. But if you expose to them that this is taking place, which is what you do with real evidence, they will not protect those folks that are then exposing them to liability.

Senator RISCH. Shawna.

Ms. BADER-BLAU. Thank you, and I think we share that analysis. I maybe would add one piece on in terms of forced labor and the connection to bribery. I was mentioning the recruiters. There are many governments around the world that are trying to experiment with getting rid of the market for illegal recruiters by regulating it and owning it, basically running the market through direct-direct government-to-government recruiting, running the industry rather than leaving it to these very diverse and unregulated markets that are run by sort of the legal mafias, and also thrive on bribery, corruption, and gangs.

Senator RISCH. Thank you. Thank you, Mr. Chairman.

The CHAIRMAN. Senator Cardin.

Senator CARDIN. Thank you, Mr. Chairman. I thank you all very much for your work. In my work with the Helsinki Commission and the OSCE, trafficking has always been a very, very high priority. And I think one of the most impressive visits I have done is to visit victims' centers in foreign countries because it shows that the community understands that those who have been trafficked are victims, and that if you need to get papers in order to be legal, you have a resource you can go to and escape the person who has trafficked you. So, I would just point out that there are ways to counter this, and that we should be looking at it.

One of the great achievements in dealing with trafficking in the United States is the Trafficking in Persons Report. It was not easy to convince the State Department that they needed to be engaged. Now, they are very proud of the work that we do in trafficking and on the TIP Report. Whenever I have an ambassador from another country or a foreign minister in my office, I always have the TIP Report, and I always go over trafficking with them and ways that they can improve in trafficking, because the issue is not just with the origin country or even the destination country, but also the transit country. So, there are different areas that you can stop the trafficking, and a war zone is one of the other three. There are other areas that can help us prevent that type of trafficking.

My first question is, How can we improve the TIP Report to deal with your concerns? I know countries do not want to be on the Tier 2 Watch List and certainly not the Tier 3, but there is waiver authority, and there is concern as to whether we can make the TIP reports even more effective, particularly dealing with trafficking and forced labor.

Mr. HAUGEN. Well, first of all, Senator, I want to thank you for carrying the TIP Report around. It is kind of a stinky document to carry around the world, but it is unbelievably powerful because governments do not want accountability and transparency for the reality within their country for this horrible crime. And yet there is nothing really like it in the world in terms of ratcheting up the pressure. I have seen governments going from not caring at all to running in a hurry to address the problem and actually changing law enforcement to respond.

I think what the TIP Report primarily needs is just enhanced stature and support from the whole U.S. Government to say this is not a document we are ashamed of. This is not a little office of the State Department that we are barely going to mention. In fact, we have been actually saying you ought to allow the TIP Office to become a full bureau so it is in the important conversations at the table where a lot of the political decisions about where pressure is going to be applied and not take place, and they are not actually in the room.

But I think strengthening the political stature of this as a priority for us is what is going to make the difference because the TIP Report has, I think, just about all the information that it needs. It can be strengthened on performance measurements of the criminal justice system I think, but that is extraordinarily strong. And what mostly needs to happen is just the stature with which our diplomatic interactions bring strength to bear on behalf of it.

Ms. BADER-BLAU. Thank you for the question, and thank you, all the Senators on this committee, for the focus on the TIP Report. It is a really important report. As a human rights activist, I would say I find the TIP Report and associated U.S. diplomacy to have the highest potential for impact on human rights than anything we do in our U.S. foreign policy. And I have actually seen that on the ground, seen the TIP Report when we focus a diplomatic effort behind the tier rankings and match it with adequate program and support on the ground make a real impact in the lives of average people. It is a very important report.

I think, you know, in terms—for us how the TIP Office could be more effective certainly with more resources, right now they are small enough that they have to really focus interventions. You know, they have got that really amazing report that covers the whole globe with fantastic suggestions at eradicating forced slavery and modern slavery and for every country in the world, and they do not have the resources to do it all. It means that they have to triage each year and do very little work compared to what they have the capacity for, so I think that would help.

Senator CARDIN. Let me go to your point that you raised on transparency in the supply chain. We looked at voluntary ways to get more transparency in different areas. In extractive industries we have the EITI, which is a voluntary way countries can come together to disclose their energy and mineral contracts so that we can trace money that should go to the country itself but may go toward corruption. We found EITI to be helpful, but it is still not enough. So in the Congress we have passed a transparency bill known as Cardin-Lugar that requires mandatory SEC filings from extractive industries.

What would you recommend in regard to transparency in the supply chain dealing with forced labor? Do we need a mandatory reporting requirement in the United States that would hopefully then be picked up by other countries so that we can get a more comprehensive view, or are you to believe that we can develop the protocols voluntarily within the business community in this regard?

Ms. BADER-BLAU. Senator Cardin, thank you. I am not a fan of voluntary reporting when it comes to something as vile as slavery and forced labor. I think it is not too much to ask, and believe that we can come up with a mandatory reporting. And I do believe that legislation would help with that.

Senator CARDIN. And I assume that the United States is going to have to lead here. If we do not do it, other countries will not take the initiative.

Ms. BADER-BLAU. The United States absolutely must take the lead on this.

Senator CARDIN. My last question deals with the opportunities under the Trans-Pacific Partnership, TPP. Malaysia is one of the TPP aspirants. They are on Tier 3 in the TIP Report. What would you expect us to be able to accomplish in successful TPP negotiations as it relates to trafficking?

Ms. BADER-BLAU. Well, I believe that thankfully we have this very strong set of recommendations in the TIP Report for Malaysia, for example. I think that we should take that like a handbook when working on this new trade agreement. Before we lose the leverage of extending the trade agreement, to work with the Government of Malaysia to make the changes that are needed and laid out in that TIP Report.

You know, for example, we work in Malaysia, and since the Tier 3 ranking came out, we have seen, on the ground, very little coming out of the government in terms of changes. They are not increasing prosecutions. They are not going after the bad actors, and they are not rescuing victims from forced labor. I do not think we should let this go. I think we should work a little harder on that, and I think we should ask for changes in advance of turning over our leverage in the TPP.

Senator CARDIN. Thank you, Mr. Chairman.

The CHAIRMAN. Thank you, and thanks for your leadership on this issue the entire time you have been in Congress, and for being here today, absolutely.

Senator Isakson.

Senator ISAKSON. I want to follow up on Senator Cardin's point and your response. You know, we found in Africa with the Millennium Challenge Corporation and the moneys that are invested in

Africa, we conditioned a lot of those investments based on a lessening of corruption and improvement in labor standards. And we have in some cases taken countries out of those programs because they would not cooperate.

When we do the TPP, one of the main things we want to do is use the leverage if these countries want to do business with the United States to have incremental improvements in the way they treat their labor and a total disregard for human trafficking. Would you agree with that?

Ms. BADER-BLAU. I believe that before we negotiate a TPP, if we put this all hard on the table, they want that agreement really badly. And I think we can use this time to say before we finish this agreement, we want to see some real steps, some real changes. We have experiences with other negotiations related to trade that the incremental approach sometimes just means incremental is 15 or 20 years.

And I think with such an extreme case like forced labor and trafficking, I think it is not too much to ask that we see real significant changes in policies and practices before we finish the negotiations.

Senator ISAKSON. And we found incremental is acceptable as long as when they violate an increment, they have a punishment for it, and they actually realize there is a consequence.

Ms. BADER-BLAU. And that is the other issue is that whether or not it is before or after, at some point we also need to monitor and enforce. And the ongoing resources for the TIP Office, the State Department and even USAID that is now trying to work across the agency to mainstream TIP through its C–TIP policy. More resources to these agencies will help monitor over time. I think that is a really important point.

Senator ISAKSON. I read your story in your testimony about the Indian woman who hired a recruiter 20 years ago to find her a job, and the recruiter found her a job in Kuwait City. She and her husband followed the recruiter to Kuwait City, and if I read it correctly, the University of Kuwait hired her, and she has for 2 years washed towels in the women's dormitory at the University of Kuwait. Was never allowed out of the building where she washed those towels, and was not allowed to see her husband.

And it occurred to me that I know traffickers take advantage of poverty, and they take advantage of weakness and illness. Are they also taking advantage of the treatment of women under Sharia law or in Islamic states where women are a second-class citizen by virtue of that religion, because Kuwait City with its great university, you would think as an employer, the university would everything to have equality for the women. But to actually be employing the woman in a substandard job, and almost holding her as a slave, is the religion a part of that? Is it cultural? What is it?

Ms. BADER-BLAU. In some ways I wish it were as easy as cultural because then we could say it would be worse in one place or another. But the reality is the condition, particularly of domestic workers, in most parts of the world is just that, and that includes countries of all different religious and ethnic backgrounds. We see this problem from Southeast Asia, across China, in the Middle East, and beyond.

The problem is really that when people employ domestic workers, they view them as people that they can lock away in the house that no one is even going to see and are at their beck and call. There is no regulation of their work. They are not even seen as workers—they are not covered by labor laws. And it is painfully common that forced labor is present in the domestic worker arena. And I would say, though, that what is common is that the majority of domestic workers around the world are women. And I do think that there is a common gender inequality issue that affects forced labor of women in domestic work.

Mr. HAUGEN. I would add a word on that, Senator, which is simply to say there are variations on cultural attitudes about treatment of women and treatment of the poor, but all these countries have put in law that slavery is not permitted. And the question is are they simply enforcing the cultural norm they have actually already embedded in the law, and the answer is ''No.'' But we can now powerfully move countries to actually enforce the cultural norm in law, and for most slaves, that will end slavery for them.

Senator ISAKSON. Following up on—since you are talking, I will follow up with one question I have for you. Every golf cap I have bought in the last 25 years was made in Bangladesh, and we have seen a tremendous movement of textiles to Asia and the Pacific region. How are our companies in America doing in terms of holding producers of those products to a higher standard in terms of their labor laws in those companies?

Mr. HAUGEN. How are U.S.——

Senator ISAKSON. How are U.S. companies who retail those products—are there any—are U.S. companies showing—shining a light on better treatment for those workers and trying to avoid doing business with people who are actually holding people in slavery?

Mr. HAUGEN. I think definitely when the United States treats it workers well, it raises the bar.

Senator ISAKSON. But I am talking about in terms of the workers in the country where the baseball caps are made, for example.

Mr. HAUGEN. Yes.

Senator ISAKSON. If an American company buys them and trademarks them, with their trademark on them, do you see evidence of United States companies putting a standard of excellence or a standard of behavior on those countries in terms of their labor laws?

Mr. HAUGEN. Yes, we do. Because that is part of their supply chain, they carry with them exposure for abuses that take place in that supply chain. And as consumers increasingly care about that, we are starting to see it bump up to the very top of boardroom discussions that that exposure exists. And it now has the opportunity to then leverage influence in those countries to actually enforce the laws against those abuses.

Senator ISAKSON. That is the point I wanted—Mr. Chairman, I wanted to make that point because—he is in a conversation with the ranking member. But I wanted to make that point for this reason. Senator Coons and I went to South Africa 2 years ago and toured some textile finishing plants that were finishing products for sale in the United States of America. And the companies, and I am not going to get into names, but the companies that were buying the finished product from those—were requiring standards of better treatment of their workers, and were using that as a marketing tool in the United States for the product they were selling. And that is where you take the paradigm of taking the advantage of poverty away and taking advantage of excellence in marketing. And so, I think that is a good point to continue to make.

Mr. HAUGEN. Yes, sir.

Senator ISAKSON. Thank you.

Ms. BADER-BLAU. If you have examples like that, I think we should raise them up. I think that is more the exception than the norm, and the truth is I think we have seen a real mixed record on companies taking responsibility for behavior down their supply chains. We see often more distancing than accountability, and I think that is one of the problems we need to solve.

Senator ISAKSON. I will get you some good information after the meeting. Thank you very much. Thank you, Mr. Chairman.

The CHAIRMAN. Thank you, Senator. Thank you.

Senator Gardner.

Senator GARDNER. Thank you, Mr. Chairman, and thank you for time and testimony today. Before this hearing, I had an opportunity to visit with the Colorado Organization for Victim Assistance. I met with them back in Colorado, and had followup with them prior to this hearing just to talk about some of the things that we see, that we hear, that we face in Colorado and our States. And in some of the—some of the information they sent, some of the articles, some of the studies that they had reported, it talked about how when it comes to human trafficking issues—this is your modern day slavery—that many of the victims and many of the foreign national trafficking victims have been assisted by the Colorado Organization for Victim Assistance, come to this country legally with guest worker visas. Is that true?

[Nonverbal response.]

Senator GARDNER. So we are not really talking about like somebody who has not come to this country illegally, who snuck through the cracks—gotten through the cracks somehow and is not accounted for, but is somebody that we know through the process. Is that the case around the world as well?

Ms. BADER-BLAU. In our estimation, for the most part, yes. People do migrate on legal visas to go from Nepal to Saudi Arabia. As a very poor person without a lot of money to buy that ticket and figure out the visa, no. They have a broker. They help them get into the country legally. The problem is the visa program itself. The visa they come in on ties them to an employer, and there is no regulation about what happens before they leave. So if they have had to pay $6,000, $8,000 illegally to a broker that they are now indebted to, sold their house, this is very common.

And then, they go to a country where they are on a legal visa program, but then something happens. The employer, because of lack of enforcement, does not pay what they are owed. They are trapped in debt bondage, and this is incredibly common.

Senator GARDNER. I think one of the challenges that we have as policymakers, as leaders in this effort to combat this, I think a lot of people think that this may be related to immigration when it is not. I mean, this is actually just—you know, in terms of documents or visas, that is not the issue. The issue is how people are treating—how we are holding people accountable.

There is a story that they shared about two brothers from Peru who came to Colorado, who were working on a sheep ranch in western Colorado. And it talked about how they were treated, how they were abused, how they had been—passports withheld, and it talks about how they escaped. It talks about this very telling story, this very emotional story about how they were able to escape, and what they did, and the fear that they lived under, and who they went to for assistance, not knowing whether their employer was going to find them and trap them back into this great tragedy again.

Are we doing enough in the United States to hold those employers accountable, to make examples? When this is reported, are we doing enough so that when we talk to other nations, when we enter into agreements, that they can look at us without hypocrisy knowing that we have done everything we have said we want them to do? Are we doing enough?

Mr. HAUGEN. If I could just respond. You have a critical insight here because it is absolutely true that the vast majority of slaves in the world are citizens within their own country. Yes, moving populations and immigration is one of those vulnerability factors, but most slaves—most of this 30 million or more slaves are citizens within their own country. So the United States will not be able to have as effective a leadership role in helping other countries in that regard if it is not doing what it can do within its own country to make sure it is enforcing laws to protect the basic rights of workers here within our borders, and holding companies accountable that violate those laws.

Senator GARDNER. Go ahead.

Ms. BADER-BLAU. I will just quickly agree and say within our guest worker visa programs, there are lots of gaps in terms of making sure that people are not coming into these programs indebted before they come, that once they come, if they face exploitation or abuse, that they are able to, without retaliation, raise unsafe working conditions or harmful employment conditions. And their ability to do that is very limited, and also being tied to employers is still a problem in the United States.

Senator GARDNER. And there have been things like the Polaris Project, which up until this past year had Colorado ranked very low in terms of its laws and protections it was providing to workers. But as a result of changes made by the State legislature, this past year rank it in the top tier, in fact, one of the States with the best laws to protect people.

When we look around the globe, though, are we able to see those kinds of changes being made in the way that we—Colorado has a law basically on the books that stated laws against trafficking, trafficking in children statute. They had that on the books, but the courts interpreted it in such a way that the person had to literally own a child victim and transfer ownership in order for them to be convicted under the statute. Now, that statute has been changed. Do we see those same kinds of legal loopholes or problems around the globe that are allowing people to get off the hook?

Mr. HAUGEN. We have reviewed the laws in scores of countries where we are operating, and there are sort of technical difficulties, improvements that could be made. But overwhelmingly, the reason that there are tens of millions of people in slavery is not because the legal scheme is inadequate. It is that the enforcement mechanism is not even attempted to be leveraged, so this is our point of focus.

And when you focus on enforcement, you do end up finding, oh, here is the hiccup in the law that needs to be addressed for us to comprehensively do this. But right now, the thing we have to wrap our minds around is that you are at greater risk of being struck by lightning than you are of actually going to jail for these crimes in the countries that have the most slaves.

Senator GARDNER. And are—I am sorry. Please.

Ms. BADER-BLAU. I would say in my experience, particularly in the Middle Eastern countries where I have worked and witnessed this issue, you know, even in a country with very weak rule of law and no focus on human rights—you can take Saudi Arabia—you are not allowed to not pay workers, I mean. And the biggest incidents of forced labor you see in a country like Saudi Arabia are employers that literally do not pay workers and force them to work for months and months and sometimes years on end. It is illegal even under Saudi law, and they are not held accountable.

Senator GARDNER. And how are we doing in terms of coordination with local law enforcement, State law enforcement, I mean, in terms of the laws international organizations, associations? How are we doing with that coordination to make sure that we have the communication available to prevent this?

Mr. HAUGEN. I think this is getting much, much better.

We have been at this for almost 20 years now, and here in the United States you have seen because of the political will expressed now to address it, the coordination of law enforcement is making it harder and harder and harder for traffickers to get away with what they are doing. But it requires sustained attention. That is the thing because it preys upon those who are politically the weakest. So it requires those of us who have more political influence just to make sure that law enforcement is prioritizing these things continuously because as soon as we take our gaze off of it, the traffickers will come right back in.

Ms. BADER-BLAU. And I would just say that I think we could do a lot better. I think that we have laws on the books that are supposed to prevent the importation of goods that are made with forced labor and child labor. They are not enforced adequately. There is not enough inspection. There was recently a—you may have seen it. In December, the Los Angeles Times wrote, I think, a five-part series on forced labor in Mexico in agriculture, and the reporters chased the supply chain all the way back up to United States supermarkets on a shoestring budget, and found endemic forced labor in agriculture in Mexico.

You know, these goods are made with forced labor and child labor, young girls as young as 12 years old, you know, picking chilies off plants that end up in our supermarkets. We should enforce these laws and make sure that does not happen.

Mr. HAUGEN. Can I just add on, the data that we have seen in the fight against terrorism to actually bring intelligence together coherently, and to mine it, and to apply analytics that allow you to chase down where the bad guys are, those same tools could be applied to the fight against slavery, but we are going to need a coordinated international effort, a fusion of data by which that crime fighting can actually take place. And that is possible now if we come together with the resources to build such a capacity.

Senator GARDNER. Thank you.

The CHAIRMAN. Thank you. Thank you very much.

Senator Rubio.

Senator RUBIO. Thank you, Mr. Chairman, for holding this hearing. At the outset, let me congratulate you for the title, "Ending Modern Slavery." That is exactly what it is. I have no problem with the term "trafficking," except I think it sometimes sanitizes what we are talking about. "Trafficking" makes it sound like people are just being moved around from point A to point B. It is not the moving around as much as what happens once they get there. And I think "modern slavery" accurately assesses it.

To that point, we have an ambassador at large for trafficking in persons—it should be an ambassador at large for ending human slavery or modern slavery—that has sat vacant for a number of— for quite a period of time. I hope that there will be a nomination and that we can get that confirmed because I think that is important in terms of the U.S.'s role around the world on this issue.

I wanted to touch on two subjects. The first is, and we had not touched on this yet, but let me ask you this. There have also been reports of abuses in the diplomatic corps here in the United States. Do you have any unique insight into some of those abuses and how they have used their diplomatic status to bring—in some instances we have seen here in Washington, to see domestic workers that are actually being not compensated and held against their will?

Mr. HAUGEN. Just to say I think it is a manifestation of the basic phenomena, which is at the highest levels this is not taken seriously as a crime, as a horror, and as something in which actual consequences must be brought to bear. And as long as it is seen that, well, wink-wink, you know, if you have the right place, if you have the right power, you can get away with this. That is what happens in the countries where the vast majority of slaves are. The people of power, of influence, they get away with it on a vast scale.

But what law brings so beautifully is equal protection of the law to say that the poorest and the richest by the law are on the same playing field, and that is the opportunity we have now is to see that these laws are actually enforced. Nothing makes that look more ridiculous than when you have these diplomatic abuses.

Ms. BADER-BLAU. Thank you for the question, and we think it is really horrific abuses we are seeing in the diplomatic corps. And I agree with Gary, it is a pretty vile practice. We understand—however, there has not been a tough enough reaction on the part of our own government to these abuses in the diplomatic corps, and sometimes it is because we have sensitive relationships with the governments in question. And that happens, as you know, with the tier rankings and the TIP Report on occasion as well.

You know, the extent to which we can de-link some of our more difficult diplomatic relationships with countries from the actual holding account to a law would be better. We understand now it may be the case that domestic workers from India will be allowed to come in again to join the diplomatic corps under a different visa category, and I think that would be something to look into.

Senator RUBIO. I know that sex trafficking and sex slavery gets a lot of attention and rightfully so. I want to talk about that. My point is that it is the labor slavery that really is still the predominant number, and it can happen anywhere. I mean, people would be shocked at how prevalent it is here domestically.

I wanted to ask you domestically for a moment in the United States about three topics. The first is on the sex slavery side. Do you have any sort of insight about how many, particularly women, but even children, obviously women. Let me focus on that first, the adult women, who are in the trade now could be considered people that are being trafficked and/or held against their will? It is my personal view that virtually all of them are one way or another because coercion is not necessarily someone holding a gun to your head or someone refusing to pay you. But things like drug addiction are used as a tool. Things like fear of escape, even psychologically. It has been my experience in the interaction I have had with law enforcement involved in this that you should consider virtually every woman in that industry as being a victim of slavery basically.

Mr. HAUGEN. I would just say that there are, you know, disagreements about this and what constitutes coercion and so forth. One of the things we do know is that if you are a minor, you cannot consent to this kind of abuse, and yet you can find plenty of minors there if you prioritize this as a proactive criminal investigative matter. And you can secondly find straight-up violence, and the evidence of it, and clarity of it, that also makes it clearly an act of coercion and a criminal act.

So, yes, there is place obviously for some disagreement, but the sad part is where there is no disagreement, but there is also not adequate enforcement of the law. And this just needs to be a priority for us community by community.

Senator RUBIO. The reason why I ask you this, and I wanted you to comment as well, Ms. Blau, there are publications in the United States that openly advertise on their pages for these services. And, in fact, the same publications, like ''Village Voice,'' that have gone on to write articles ridiculing this whole notion that there is human slavery in the United States—that there is slavery in the United States with regards to the sex trade. And there has been all sorts of actions taken here to condemn that.

And the reason why I ask you that question is because oftentimes when law enforcement interacts, for example, with women that are being—that are in prostitution and have, in my opinion, been coerced into it either through drug addiction, abuse, or a combination thereof, there is a debate within the law enforcement community about whether they should be treated as perpetrators or as victims. And we have had this debate in Florida as well.

When you interact with someone that you basically have found at a brothel or, in some instances, some of these massage parlors and so forth, the debate has been should we arrest them, and put them in jail, and treat them as a perpetrator, or should we pull them out of that environment, put them into a safe place where they can realize that there is an escape for them, and they can break that pattern. And we have gotten a lot of pushback from both law enforcement and prosecutorial agencies who believe that it is important to treat them as a perpetrator first, that that is the only way you are going to get them see differently.

Do you have an opinion on the right way to address that, because it has been—it is an issue of controversy in the law enforcement community?

Mr. HAUGEN. I will state a clear preference, that the preference and better law enforcement way to approach this is to actually treat them as victims. You will get their cooperation. You will be able to get behind the real criminal networks and activities that are behind it. And I do think from my own law enforcement experience, it is a bit of a sloppy excuse to pretend that that is not possible.

Ms. BADER-BLAU. And I think we need a very robust program of training of law enforcement on this issue. And it is not just in the United States, it is globally. We have had programs that we have done in other countries, Indonesia and other places, where we have worked law enforcement to identify people that otherwise look, according to the laws, as they are perpetrating a law, to a violation of a law, such as in the commercial sex industry to identify them as victims by asking them questions. How did you get here? Where did you come from? How old are you?

The truth is I believe that many cases of labor trafficking originally end up in sex trafficking, and we find that if law enforcement can actually be trained on talking to people and understanding where they come from, that we can get more prosecutions, and we can really focus our ire where it belongs on the traffickers, and not the victims.

Senator RUBIO. I know I am out of time. In your experience, the majority of people from abroad that are here in the commercial sex industry, did they know they were coming to that industry when they were brought?

Ms. BADER-BLAU. I do not have a particular stat on that.

Senator RUBIO. Okay.

Mr. HAUGEN. In my experience, the majority are victims of coercion and fraud.

Senator RUBIO. False pretense. They thought they were coming here to make a commercial product, and they ended up trapped in this industry.

Mr. HAUGEN. Correct.

Senator RUBIO. Thank you.

The CHAIRMAN. Thank you. You all have been outstanding witnesses. In my opening comments I mentioned the role Congress has played. But, I think because of your efforts and so many advocates from around our country, the administration, too, I think is very focused on this. I know Secretary Kerry recently referred to a much more robust effort. So I think this is something that we can all work on together in a very positive way, and I want to thank you both for a lifetime of effort in this regard, for being here today, for sharing your experiences, and for working with us in the future. Thank you very much.

And now we will have the second panel. Do we have our second panel?

Mr. ABRAMOWITZ. Yes. Sorry, Mr. Chairman. They were just out in the hall doing an interview with CNN, so they are just waiting for them to clear, and they will be right in. I told them they had to mention your name, Mr. Chairman, and Senator Menendez if they were going to do this interview in your hearing, but I do not know if that happened.

The CHAIRMAN. They get mentioned enough, thank you.

Senator MENENDEZ. That is a former congressional staffer. [Laughter.]

The CHAIRMAN. We will now turn to our witnesses for the second panel. Thank you for being here. Our first witness is Mr. James Kofi Annan. In 2013, he was awarded the World's Children Prize for his work to stop child slavery. He himself was a fishing slave as a child for 7 years. He managed to escape, get an education, and become a bank manager. In 2007 he left the bank to work solely to stop child slavery. By that time, he had already started an organization called Challenging Heights in 2003, which has liberated over 500 children from slavery.

Liberated slave children come first through Challenging Heights' safe home for 65 children. Challenging Heights also runs a school for 700 pupils of different ages. They offer training to poor mothers so that they can support their families and do not just sell their children into slavery. He has supported over 10,000 children who have been slaves or at risk for slavery. Thank you for being here.

Our second witness is Shandra Woworuntu, the founder of a non-profit organization dedicated to empowering human trafficking survivors through mentorship and job training. She graduated from college with a major in finance and bank management in her native Indonesia. After graduation, she became the manager of the Treasury Department of the Korea Exchange Bank in Indonesia, specializing in money market trading.

When political turbulence erupted, she lost her job because of economic, religious, and racial persecution. She applied for a job that promised a 6-month position in the hotel industry in Chicago, which led her to become—and to survive being—a victim of a criminal human trafficking organization. Thank you again for being here today.

Our next witness is David Abramowitz. He is vice president of policy in government relations at Humanity United, a foundation that focuses on advancing human freedom by combating human trafficking and modern slavery, among other human rights issues. Previously he served as Department of State's Office of Legal Advisor.

In 1999, he joined the staff of the Committee on Foreign Affairs for the House of Representatives, and served as chief counsel. Over the next year 10 years, he worked on such legislation as the Victims of Trafficking and Violence Act of 2000 and the William Wilberforce Trafficking Victims Protection Reauthorization Act of 2008.

And with that, we will recognize James Kofi Annan. If you would begin and just go in order. Thank you all for being here.

STATEMENT OF JAMES KOFI ANNAN, FOUNDER, CHALLENGING HEIGHTS, KANESHI, ACCRA, GHANA

Mr. ANNAN. Thank you, Chairman Corker, Senator Menendez, and other members of the committee for holding this important hearing. I am the founder of Challenging Heights, an organization that for 10 years has helped children who have been trafficked into modern slavery in Ghana. We deliver social justice interventions to children, women, and underserved communities in coastal and farming communities. Our work includes rescue, rehabilitation, and reintegration of children who have been trafficked into the fishing industry. We also raise awareness of trafficking in communities to prevent trafficking and re-trafficking of children.

In fishing communities along the lake, Ghanaian children are being sold into a life of forced labor, malnutrition, abuse, and no school. Traffickers prey on poor families in communities along the country's coast. Typically, families are told by their traffickers that if they let their children come to the lake, they will live with relatives who will care for them and send them to school in exchange for a few hours of work after school. In reality, the children are forced to work long hours on their boats and in dangerous conditions.

A typical day might begin at 3 a.m. and end at 8 p.m., and include challenging tasks such as casting nets, diving, hauling, with only one meal served. Children often get stuck in the nets at the bottom of the lake as a result of unsafe diving. If a child is caught escaping, the consequences can be brutal. Often the families do not hear from their children again.

I founded Challenging Heights because I was a victim of this slavery situation myself. I was forced to work in the fishing boats on Lake Volta as a young child. I understood the challenge of surviving such a trauma, and I also saw the tremendous potential to change things in my country to prevent child labor, to rescue children from slavery, and to give those survivors a chance for a good life.

Our organization supports hundreds of children and their families each year. We help prevent trafficking by helping vulnerable children to go to school, by creating awareness, building communities' capacity to stand up against trafficking. We also have a survivors' rehabilitation center and a child trafficking survivor support network aimed at providing protection for children.

I am very proud of my organization's accomplishments, but I know that there is so much more we need to do to stop trafficking in Ghana and throughout Africa. The U.S. Government plays an important role in this direction. The U.S. State Department's Trafficking in Persons Report issued each year is a useful tool for Ghana and other governments, helping to keep them accountable for continuing to do better work to stop trafficking. Each year I contribute to the report so it reflects the most up-to-date reality facing trafficking survivors in Ghana. And just a couple of days ago I was sent information to start making my input. I host U.S. Government officials, showing them firsthand the dire situation facing children at risk of exploitation.

The United States diplomatic pressure is very important in helping to persuade the Government of Ghana to act. It is critical that these efforts continue and are properly funded. In particular, we would like to see a renewal of commitment to the National Plan of Action, which the government itself has created, and money allocated to the Human Trafficking Board to be released for immediate use.

The Department of Labor's Bureau of International Labor Affairs also plays an important role in combating trafficking in Ghana and other countries. First, it conducts research on international labor, forced labor, and human trafficking, and publishes very valuable reports that help hold countries accountable. The Bureau funds projects for organizations and engages in efforts to eliminate exploitative child labor around the world. And lastly, it assists in the development and implementation of U.S. Government policy on international labor, forced labor, and human trafficking issues.

This important bureau must retain its resources and expertise to address the most intractable forms of child labor and exploitation. I urge Congress to consider legislation that would secure permanent resources for ILAB and insulate it from political shifts. I also believe that the U.S. Government can improve implementation of its development programs. Whether it is building a school, constructing a highway, or distributing food aid, the U.S. Government must integrate strategies for preventing, identifying, and responding to trafficking.

It is especially important that development programs fund projects that focus on prevention of slavery, and I will specifically cite the example of the Millennium Challenge Account, which we believe can be tied to some of these issues of slavery. Ideally, the government should target resources toward grassroots organizations as Ghanaians themselves and those in other countries struggling to end human trafficking are the only ones who can do the difficult work of changing attitudes in their own countries.

Thank you, Mr. Chairman.

[The prepared statement of Mr. Annan follows:]

PREPARED STATEMENT OF JAMES KOFI ANNAN

Thank you, Chairman Corker, Senator Menendez, and other members of the committee for holding this important hearing to consider how fight modern slavery, a most horrific human rights crime.

I am the founder of Challenging Heights, an organization that for nearly 12 years has served children who have been trafficked into modern slavery in the Lake Volta region of Ghana. Our organization delivers social justice interventions to children, women, and underserved communities in coastal and farming communities. Our work includes rescue, rehabilitation, and reintegration of children who have been trafficked in the fishing industry, as well as creating community awareness on these issues in order to prevent trafficking and re-trafficking of children.

Challenging Heights also contributes to policy and awareness creation and the public discourse on issues affecting Ghanaian children. Additionally, the organization runs a school for more than 700 children who are survivors of child trafficking or who are at risk of child trafficking.

The question you are asking today: What is the best way forward to ending modern slavery? That is a very big and important question. I believe the answer has many facets, just as human trafficking takes so many forms.

In fishing communities along Lake Volta, Ghanaian children are being sold into a life of forced labor, malnutrition, abuse, and no schooling. Traffickers prey on poor families in communities along the country's coast. Typically, the families are told by the trafficker that if they let their children come to the lake they will live with relatives who will care for them and send them to school in exchange for a few hours' work after school. In reality, the children are forced to work long hours on the boats in dangerous conditions. A typical day might begin at 3 a.m. and end at

8 p.m. and include challenging tasks such as casting nets, diving, and hauling, with only one meal served. Children often get stuck in the nets at the bottom of the lake. If a child is caught escaping, the consequences can be brutal. Often the families do not hear from their children again.

I formed Challenging Heights because I was a child slave myself who was forced to work in the fishing boats on Lake Volta as a young boy. I understood the challenge of surviving such a trauma, and I also saw the tremendous potential to change things in my country, to prevent child labor, to rescue children from slavery and to give those survivors a chance for a good life.

Today, Challenging Heights supports hundreds of children and their families each year. We help prevent human trafficking from taking place by helping vulnerable children go to school, creating awareness and building community capacity to stand up against trafficking. We also have a 65-capacity survivors' rehabilitation center, and a child trafficking survivors support network aimed at providing protection for children.

I feel proud of our accomplishments, but I know that there is so much more we need to do to stop trafficking in Ghana and throughout Africa. The United States Government plays an important role.

First, the U.S. State Department's Trafficking in Persons Report issued each year is a useful tool for Ghana and other governments, helping to keep them accountable for continuing to do better work to stop trafficking. Each year I contribute to the report so it reflects the most up to date reality facing trafficking survivors in Ghana. I host U.S. Government officials, showing them firsthand the dire situation facing children at risk of exploitation.

The United States diplomatic pressure is very important in helping to persuade the Government of Ghana to act. It is critical that these efforts continue and are properly funded. In particular we would like to see a renewal of commitment to the National Plan of Action, and money allocated to the Human Trafficking Board released for immediate use.

The Department of Labor's Bureau of International Labor Affairs (ILAB) also plays an important role. The Bureau does a number of important things that affect trafficking in Ghana and other countries:

(1) It conducts research on international child labor, forced labor, and human trafficking and publishes very valuable reports on the worst incidences of child labor, and lists of goods produced by child labor and forced labor;

(2) The Bureau funds projects for organizations engaged in efforts to eliminate exploitive child labor around the world; and

(3) It assists in the development and implementation of U.S. Government policy on international child labor, forced labor, and human trafficking issues.

One thing I am concerned about is that this important Bureau retains its resources and expertise to address the most intractable forms of child labor and exploitation. Even as gains are made in reducing the prevalence of child labor worldwide, real and complex problems remain. I believe Congress should consider legislation that would secure permanent resources for the Bureau of International Labor Affairs and insulate it from political shifts.

I also believe that the U.S. Government can improve the implementation of all its development programs by integrating an antitrafficking lens. Whether it is building a school, constructing a highway, or distributing food aid, the U.S. Government must integrate strategies for preventing, identifying, and responding to trafficking. It is especially important that development programs fund projects that focus on prevention of slavery. Ideally, the government should target resources toward grassroots organizations, as Ghanaians themselves—and those in other countries struggling to end human trafficking—are the only ones who can do the difficult work of changing attitudes in their own communities.

Mr. Chairman, thank you for the opportunity to share my perspective, and for this committee's work to find a way to end modern slavery.

The CHAIRMAN. Thank you very much.

Ms. Woworuntu.

STATEMENT OF SHANDRA WOWORUNTU, TRAFFICKING SURVIVOR, NEW YORK, NY

Ms. WOWORUNTU. Thank you, Chairman Corker, Senator Menendez, and other members of the Foreign Relations Committee for holding this hearing today. I am an advocate, a survivor of human trafficking, and the founder of Mentari, a nonprofit organization dedicated to providing human trafficking survivors with mentorship and job training to help them rebuild their lives.

In my native Indonesia, I was a college-educated financial analyst employed by an international bank. I lost my job in 1998 because of political turbulence and its fallout, so I expanded my job search to the United States. And after I responded to advertisement for a job in a hotel in Chicago, I checked my legal documents, paid a $3,000 recruitment fee, accepted the position, and I flew to New York City.

I entered the United States lawfully on a nonimmigrant visa arranged through the recruitment agency that brought me here. I was picked up at the airport with five other women, and soon our passports were forcibly taken, and our lives threatened. And the abusive situation become clear: we were being trafficked into the sex trade. And they asked me to pay $30,000 U.S. to be free.

I managed to escape, and I cooperated with law enforcement to successfully prosecute my trafficker, and we rescued many girls. It was hard for me to survive because there were not many services available to help me. Safe Horizon in New York assisted me to stay legally in the United States.

I believe to end human trafficking globally, the U.S. Government needs to focus on prevention and strengthening policies to prosecute the traffickers, and to provide victims with stable and sustainable support. And I also believe that policymakers should listen to the voices and opinions of survivors of human trafficking. And I thank you for doing that today.

One of the best ways to prevent human trafficking is through education and awareness. I urge Congress to invest in supporting and encouraging countries to implement programs that will make people more aware, and will help them question whether a job opportunity is legitimate or the work of criminal labor recruiters, like the one I met in Indonesia. Labor recruiter and contractors are directly involved in the trafficking and exploitation of workers around the world. Criminal recruiters make false promises about the job, and charge workers high recruitment fees that force workers to stay in abusive or exploitive working conditions under debt bondage.

Mr. Chairman, last year Congress considered, but did not pass, the Fraudulent Overseas Recruitment and Trafficking Elimination, or FORTE, Act of 2013. I urge you to support introduction and passage of similar legislation this year. This will require that workers coming to the United States receive accurate information about the job and working condition they are being offered, and would also ensure that workers do not have to pay recruitment fees.

Another important step Congress can take to prevent human trafficking is to demand transparency in supply chains for products that are sold in United States. California passed legislation that requires companies to publicly disclose what efforts, if any, they are taking to ensure the supply chains do not include forced labor. Congress should support supply chain transparency on the Federal level, and Congresswoman Carolyn Maloney has introduced the Business Supply Chains Transparency on Human Trafficking and Slavery Act in the House to achieve this goal.

I also urge Congress to strengthen the United States role in developing a shared global foreign policy and especially to prosecute the traffickers. Building our capacity to conduct intercountry investigations and prosecution should be high priority in that effort.

Mr. Chairman, I want also to ask today for your support for a Senate companion to H.R. 500, the Survivors of Human Trafficking Empowerment Act. This bill will create a survivor-led U.S. advisory council on human trafficking to review Federal Government policy programs on human trafficking. And it is so important that survivors play a role in finding solutions to end modern slavery. This proposed legislation is a great step forward.

I want to close by saying something about human trafficking survivors. It is very difficult for survivors to recover from such a terrible experience. It is challenging when you are in a country where you do not speak the language and have little or no support. I hope the U.S. Government will recognize the need to provide sustainable support for survivors, including long-term support, to help survivors receive training and opportunities to gain employment. I believe United States can and should be a leader in demonstrating the best practice to the world.

Thank you.

[The prepared statement of Ms. Woworuntu follows:]

PREPARED STATEMENT OF SHANDRA WOWORUNTU

Thank you, Chairman Corker, Senator Menendez and other members of the Foreign Relations Committee for holding this hearing on how we can move forward to end modern slavery.

I am an advocate, a survivor of human trafficking, and the founder of Mentari, a nonprofit organization dedicated to providing human trafficking survivors with mentorship and job training to help them rebuild their lives.

In my native Indonesia, I was a college-educated financial analyst employed by an international bank. I lost my job in 1998 because of political turbulence and its fallout, so I expanded my job search to the United States. After responding to an advertisement for a job in a Chicago hotel, I checked the legal documents, paid a recruiter fee, accepted the position, and flew to New York City.

I entered the United States lawfully on a nonimmigrant visa arranged through the "recruiting organization" that brought me here. I was picked up at the airport, along with five other women, by men we all believed were affiliated with our recruiter. Shortly thereafter, however, our passports were forcibly removed, our lives were threatened and the situation became clear: we were being trafficked into the sex trade.

I managed to escape by jumping out of a small bathroom window, and I cooperated with law enforcement to successfully prosecute my trafficker. It was hard for me to survive because there were not many services available to help me. Safe Horizon, NY assisted me to be independent and also to stay legally in the United States.

I believe that to end human trafficking globally, the U.S. Government needs to focus on prevention, and on strengthening policies that are enacted to prosecute traffickers, and to provide victims with stable and sustainable support.

The U.S. Government has been a leader, through its annual Trafficking in Persons report and other diplomatic initiatives, in urging governments around the world to do a better job of preventing modern slavery. Our government can do much more.

One of the most effective ways to prevent human trafficking is through education and awareness. I urge Congress to invest in supporting and encouraging countries to implement programs that will make people more aware, and will help them question whether a job opportunity is legitimate, or the work of a criminal labor recruiter.

Labor recruiters and contractors are directly involved in the trafficking and exploitation of workers around the world, including men, women, and children who enter the United States lawfully. These criminal recruiters make false promises about jobs and charge workers high recruitment fees that force workers to stay in abusive or exploitative working conditions under debt bondage.

I know several trafficking survivors who paid up to $20,000 in recruitment fees for jobs that didn't exist. In most cases, they borrowed the money from people or loan sharks in their home country that expect to be paid back. Now exploited, trafficked, and unpaid, they cannot pay back those loans—this creates debt bondage.

It is important to have uniform standards for employment agencies that send workers to another country. They should be required to give information about the working conditions for the jobs they are offering, and they should provide workers with a clear description of the workers' rights.

Congress has an opportunity to help prevent trafficking by illicit labor recruiters into the United States, and to demonstrate to other countries the kind of policies needed to address human trafficking. I urge Congress to reintroduce The Fraudulent Overseas Recruitment and Trafficking Elimination (FORTE) Act of 2013, which would deter human trafficking, forced labor and exploitation by:

1. Requiring that workers coming to the United States receive accurate information about the job, their visa, and working conditions;
2. Ensuring that no fees for recruitment are charged to workers;
3. Requiring that the recruitment agency registers with the Department of Labor; and
4. Enforcing a penalty if the law is not followed.

I encounter men and women from all over the world who have experienced human trafficking in some form. They are from different nations, cultures, and backgrounds, but many have one thing in common: they were brought here by a seemingly reputable recruiting agency. With an estimated 14,000 individuals trafficked into this country each year, it's a problem that needs to be addressed—this legislation is one important part of the solution.

Another important step that the U.S. Government can take to prevent modern slavery is to demand transparency in supply chains for products that are sold in the United States. California has passed legislation that requires companies to publicly disclose what efforts, if any, they are taking to ensure their supply chains do not include forced labor. This legislation is a good first step, but it should not be limited to one state; Congress should initiate supply chain transparency on a national level.

I also urge Congress to strengthen the United States role in developing a shared global foreign policy to fight human trafficking, and especially to prosecute traffickers. Building our capacity to conduct intercountry investigation and prosecutions should be a high priority in that effort.

Mr. Chairman, I want to ask today for your support of a Senate companion to H.R. 500, the Survivors of Human Trafficking Empowerment Act, introduced by Representatives Honda and Poe. This bill would create a survivors-led U.S. Advisory Council on Human Trafficking to review Federal Government policy and programs on human trafficking. It is so important that survivors play a role in finding the solutions to end modern slavery, and in helping the government understand how to provide survivors the support they need. This proposed legislation is a great step forward.

I want to close by saying that as a survivor of human trafficking, I am committed to empowering other survivors. That is why I established Mentari, an organization based in New York that provides mentorship and job training to survivors. It is very difficult for trafficking survivors in the United States, and globally, to recover from such a terrible experience. It is even more challenging when you are in a country where you don't speak the language and have little or no family support. I hope the U.S. Government will recognize the need to provide sustainable support for survivors, including long-term support to help survivors receive training and opportunities to gain employment. Programs that support job training and job creation can help prevent survivors from being retrafficked, as well as protect all men and women who are vulnerable to exploitation and trafficking. I believe the United States, again, can and should be a leader in demonstrating best practices to the world.

The CHAIRMAN. Thank you very much.

Mr. Abramowitz.

STATEMENT OF DAVID ABRAMOWITZ, VICE PRESIDENT, POLICY AND GOVERNMENT RELATIONS, HUMANITY UNITED, WASHINGTON, DC

Mr. ABRAMOWITZ. Thank you, Mr. Chairman, and thank you, Mr. Menendez, Mr. Chairman, and members of the committee, for holding this very important hearing. And thanks for the opportunity to testify today. Mr. Chairman, Humanity United combats modern slavery by building effective networks, engaging the private sector, and strengthening the antislavery advocacy movement, including support for the Alliance to End Slavery and Trafficking.

Mr. Chairman, as you said, with two-thirds or more of the profits for modern slavery coming from sex trafficking and two-thirds of the victims subject to labor trafficking, we must work urgently to combat human trafficking in all its forms.

Each of these victims, Mr. Chairman, deserves to become a survivor, and I feel privileged to be testifying alongside two of them today. I think the kind of testimony and experiences they can bring demonstrate why the legislation that Ms. Woworuntu just mentioned on having the survivor advisory council is very important so that the executive branch could really hear in a very specific way from survivors moving forward.

Mr. Chairman, turning to more specific solutions, I first want to focus on foreign labor recruiters. A lot has been said about that. We heard a lot about it from the last panel as well as the panel here. In my testimony, I talk about the whole system of foreign labor recruiting, including corruption, which I think Senator Risch was very correct in terms of identifying that as a key issue. But there are a number of ways that we can address it.

First, these issues have to come out more in the open with a more frank discussion. The TIP Report was mentioned earlier and also in the testimony of my fellow panelists. It can really bring a lot of information to light. It can help identify which countries are the key countries that need to be focused on. It can analyze the commitment of those governments trying to end human trafficking, where perhaps more pressure needs to be brought. And it also points out sensible solutions.

But this report is only as valuable as it is accurate, and as Senator Rubio pointed out, we have had a vacancy in the TIP ambassador slot. We are about to start the report season where the information that James and others are going to provide will start to be looked at. And I am very worried that if we do not have someone in that position, then those who want to downplay abuses in certain countries are likely to be successful, and we will not have a report that has as much integrity as in the past. And I would ask unanimous consent that a piece that I just wrote in The Hill on this matter, which lays out certain criteria for a new Ambassador, be put in the record.

Second, Mr. Chairman, governments can require greater transparency and regulate foreign labor recruiters. The FORTE Act that Shandra just mentioned is very important. It lays out transparency, bans fees, and creates a regulatory structure. And we also have the Executive Order 13627 on strengthening protections against trafficking persons in Federal contracts, which has similar provisions. And this committee really needs to make sure that that Executive order is implemented. One of the most important reasons to do so is U.S. leadership. If we can demonstrate that we are trying to dive down into these issues, then it gives us much better moral authority to try to address these issues with other governments.

Third, technology can play a role in providing worker information. One such platform that has recently been developed is Contratados. Think of this as the mobile application Yelp, but for foreign labor recruiters and for companies. It allows workers to rate companies and employers and to warn other workers of bad experiences.

A lot was said about supply chains. The work is hard to look at these supply chains, and we can try to help companies think about their supply chains. For example, the Coalition for Immokalee Workers that was mentioned by Ms. Bader-Blau, works directly with workers, growers, corporations to together eliminate slavery and the sexual abuse that comes with it from tomato fields in Florida.

Technology and big data was mentioned. Verite, which is a leader in issues looking at labor, and Palantir Technologies, which is a big data analytics company that is used across many areas of law enforcement, are partnering to pilot a potentially transformative analytical product that will enable companies to unravel complex labor supply chains and identify risks of human trafficking and forced labor.

There are other kinds of private sector and civil society partnerships that can work across sectors. For example, in the sustainability area, there is a lot of work that has been done to try to prevent rain forests from being cut down in order to preserve the rain forests.

However, there is also forced labor and modern slavery that are engaged with both the cutting of the forests and then the palm plantations that are planted in their place. If we can bring these siloed communities together to work together, they can try to make real progress in this area.

Similarly, Mr. Chairman, we in Humanity United are working in Nepal with brick kiln owners. We are trying to provide them incentives so that they can both reduce emissions and also end child labor. However, we have to be careful about the unintended consequences of our actions as workers can return to their village into the same cycle of poverty and exploitation. Small investments in education and livelihood, as we just heard, can make our efforts to free slaves sustainable. That is why baseline measurements and strong evaluation and monitoring are critical to ensure that the interventions are actually reducing modern slavery as opposed to just displacing it.

I go through, Mr. Chairman, in my testimony a number of others matters regarding partnerships, including the way the corporate sector can work with law enforcement in order to try to eliminate human trafficking through the data that they collect. But we really need to bring together private donors, governments, the private sector, civil society, and survivors together.

In conclusion, Mr. Chairman, and Senator Menendez, and other members of the committee, last week marked the 150th year since the House of Representatives voted to approve the 13th Amendment ending slavery in the United States. This coming December we will mark the adoption of the amendment as the law of the land. This committee can play a really instrumental leadership role in helping mark that anniversary by pushing forward the fight against human trafficking and modern slavery.

Thank you, Mr. Chairman.

[The prepared statement of Mr. Abramowitz follows:]

PREPARED STATEMENT OF DAVID S. ABRAMOWITZ

Mr. Chairman, Senator Menendez, and distinguished members of the committee, thank you for holding this hearing on one of the most terrible human rights abuses of our times—the widespread occurrence of human trafficking and modern slavery—and thank you for the opportunity to testify today.

Mr. Chairman, I am the Vice President of Policy and Government Relations at Humanity United, a U.S.-based foundation dedicated to building peace and advancing human freedom. Over the past decade, Humanity United has worked to combat human trafficking and end modern day slavery in the United States and around the globe.

We do this by building effective networks to address this issue, raising awareness, encouraging sustained government leadership on the issue, engaging the private sector to become part of the solution, and by strengthening and supporting the anti-slavery advocacy movement.

In that context, we support the Alliance to End Slavery and Trafficking, a coalition of 14 U.S.-based human rights organizations that advocates for solutions to prevent and end all forms of human trafficking and modern slavery around the world. The coalition presses for lasting solutions to prevent labor and sex trafficking, hold perpetrators accountable, ensure justice for victims, and empower survivors with tools for recovery.

SCOPE AND NATURE OF TRAFFICKING IN PERSONS AND MODERN DAY SLAVERY

Mr. Chairman, human trafficking and modern slavery inflict enormous human suffering. While data collection on this underground crime is challenging, we know that tens of millions of people around the globe are subject to this abuse, and conservative estimates put global profits at $150 billion.[1] It is one of the most pressing and complex human rights challenges of our time, yet also crosses over into such diverse areas as transnational crime, international humanitarian law, domestic and international labor frameworks, and migration, among others.

And we know that human trafficking and modern slavery has many faces. Exploited through force, fraud, or coercion, these are adults and children who are forced to work on fishing vessels, in mines, plantations, sweatshops, and brothels. Two thirds of the profits from modern slavery come from sex trafficking, while two-thirds of the victims are in labor trafficking.[2] We must work urgently to combat human trafficking in all its forms.

Mr. Chairman, this is not a matter of numbers: each individual story of this suffering and exploitation is a human rights tragedy that violates our values and beliefs. As you know, modern slavery is also not a far away problem that only affects distant lands. It remains a shock to most Americans but thousands of adults are trafficked into forced or exploitative labor right here in the United States. Some estimates suggest that as many as 300,000 U.S. children and youth are at risk of being trafficked into the commercial sex trade.[3] Moreover, the problem is not going away. The National Human Trafficking Resource Center hotline received nearly four times as many calls in 2013 as in 2008, with calls rising from 5,748 in 2008 to 20,579 in 2013.[4] Government-funded research also suggests that there are significant numbers of cases of labor trafficking in the United States. Extrapolating from prevalence rates in San Diego, California, one DOJ-funded study estimates that there may be nearly 2½ million workers who are victimized by traffickers.[5]

We have also learned that the sometimes-divisive dichotomy between sex and labor trafficking is an unhelpful lens for examining this phenomenon. Those exploited for labor often find themselves facing sexual abuse, which can also be a driver of vulnerability. When I was in Nepal in 2010, service providers suggested that the figure for such dual exploitation may be as high as 90 percent of those who have migrated, a figure I found shocking.

LIFTING SURVIVOR VOICES

Each of these victims, Mr. Chairman, deserves to become a survivor. They deserve the assurance that they and their families will be protected, their perpetrators will be convicted, and the trafficking of others will be prevented. And we need to support them to raise their own voices.

This is why I feel extremely privileged to be testifying with two survivors of human trafficking. Shandra Woworuntu and James Kofi Annan have faced such abuse, and through their personal strength and determination have become inspirational leaders in this fight. Pierre and Pam Omidyar, who founded and fund Humanity United, are true believers that we can only achieve sustainable social change if we work alongside those who have been or are on the front lines. So I commend you, Mr. Chairman, and you, Senator Menendez, for making sure that their voices continue to be heard.

In that connection, Mr. Chairman, I strongly recommend that you and your colleagues from the Judiciary Committee introduce and sponsor a companion to H.R. 500, the Survivors of Human Trafficking Empowerment Act, introduced by Representatives Honda and Poe in the House. This bill would ensure survivor voices are heard within the executive branch as it formulates policies to combat modern slavery. All our efforts in the United States and globally must be informed by survivors, as well as civil society.

ADDRESSING THE CHALLENGE OF ABUSES IN FOREIGN LABOR RECRUITING AND SUPPLY CHAINS

Mr. Chairman, turning to solutions, I first want to discuss is the need for governments and the business community to address the issue of foreign labor recruiters—one of the leading drivers of the phenomenon of slavery and trafficking today. Using promises of high salaries and fake job offers, unregulated and unscrupulous labor brokers can induce people to migrate thinking that they are going for legal work, only to trap them in modern slavery. We have heard from both Ms. Bader-Blau and most poignantly from Ms. Woworuntu about these challenges.

In this regard, let me make a few brief points. Mr. Chairman, it has become clear that exploitation is not only occurring in the brothels of Phnom Penh or in the rice mills of southern India. It is happening as labor recruiters and brokers supply workers to the palm oil plantations of Malaysia and to construction projects in the Persian Gulf. It is happening in the shrimp peeling shacks in Thailand and fishing vessels off its shores. It is happening as recruiters deceive young women and men with promises of legitimate work only to bind them into sexual exploitation.

The coercion and fraud used in these cases include a wide range of abuses, often in different combinations. Unregulated labor recruiters lure men and women with promises of legitimate and lucrative jobs in distant locations or foreign countries. The prospective workers typically pay exorbitant fees equal to 4–6 months of salary to middlemen for connecting them to potential jobs and for visa expenses, travel documents, transportation, health screenings, and ongoing expenses like housing and food. Recruiters are often paid twice for supplying workers to companies—once by the company that needs the workforce and once by the worker who is desperate to get the job. Workers typically borrow money to pay recruitment fees, and the terms of workers' debts make them unable to repay their loans, particularly since the job often does not pay the salary they were promised, or is something altogether different from what they were told they would do. And of course, as we heard today, recruiters sometimes place individuals in totally different situations, including in the sex trade.

Once at their destination, foreign workers may have their identity and travel documents seized, be threatened with deportation into danger, and be subjected to life-threatening conditions, confinement, and of course terrible violence. Debts can be used to ensure workers remain desperate for long work hours, no matter the conditions and, along with lack of income and deduction for fees they never knew about, lead the workers to be vulnerable to threats against them and their families at home.

Moreover, corruption plays a significant role in modern slavery and the recruitment system. In the country of origin or destination, or sometimes both, recruiters bribe government officials to look the other way. In the worst cases, government officials may come from the recruitment industry itself, and police or other security forces can be part of the scheme of coercion, lending the threat of the state to the threat of the trafficker. The challenges presented by this corruption should not be underestimated, reflecting a conspiracy between foreign officials and the labor brokers and employers who pay them off. In this cycle, many workers who have lawfully issued visas end up in modern slavery, undermining the immigration systems in destination countries.

Fortunately, international reporting is making this cycle more apparent. In last year's Trafficking in Persons (TIP) Report, for example, the State Department laid out much of this coercive cycle with respect to Thailand and the seafood sector. The report describes the brutal conditions in the industry and the abuses perpetrated on legal migrants, illegal migrants, and minorities. Between the TIP Report and the international reporting on abuses in the seafood industry, companies in Europe and the United States are coming to the table, but the right protections and systems to address abuses have yet to emerge. Thailand is just one example of where the TIP Report can help to identify a key country of need, analyze foreign government commitment to combating human trafficking and modern slavery, and point out sensiblesolutions.

Abuses like those in the Thai fishing industry are often the result of a lack of information for those who are seeking jobs to improve their lives. If prospective workers only know what they are being told by the labor recruiters who intend to exploit them, they are left to choose between the immediate prospect of a better life and often vague warnings that something may happen to them. Left with a choice between a seemingly tangible improvement for them and their families and a distant risk that something may go wrong, they tend to choose hope over fear, often to their great detriment.

Beyond increased transparency, there are numerous potential solutions to these challenges. One approach is to require greater transparency and regulate foreign labor recruiters such as those included in Chairman Ed Royce's H.R.3344—Fraudulent Overseas Recruitment and Trafficking Elimination Act of 2013. This legislation:

- Provides for transparency in contracts and its terms.
- Prohibits fees for recruitment.
- Requires foreign labor recruiters to register with the Department of State and authorizes the Department to require a bond.
- Provides a safe harbor to companies that use authorized recruiters.
- Creates enforcement mechanisms against recruiters that violate the provisions of the law.

A number of these provisions were adopted in the recently promulgated regulations to implement Executive Order 13627, Strengthening Protections Against Trafficking in Persons in Federal Contracts. As the largest single purchaser in the world, full implementation of these regulations could see a cleansing of exploitation and abuse in the supply chains of many U.S. Government suppliers. This ensures taxpayer money does not unintentionally prop up what is already the booming industry of human trafficking. I urge Congress to provide the funding needed to implement these regulations and to ensure that the U.S. Government implements them fully.

One reason to support the legislative approach and to make sure the implementation of the Executive order works is that such a law and the Executive order itself could serve as a model for other countries.

Because a government and regulatory framework can still be subject to manipulation and corruption by traffickers, another needed approach is to develop better information and more transparent processes for the workers themselves. We know the power of data and the impact of transparency to help us make better decisions. With the rapid adoption of mobile technology and the increasing penetration of mobile devices, new technological solutions are possible.

One such platform has recently been developed: Contratados.[6] Think of this as the mobile application Yelp but designed for workers to review labor recruiters and employers. This technology allows workers to rate recruitment companies and employers, and to warn other workers of bad experiences. Developed by Centro de los Derechos del Migrante, a transnational migrant rights organization based in Mexico, this type of worker facing platform holds significant promise in equipping migrants with information to make their decisions and migration safer. Humanity United is exploring such technological approaches to better protect migrants around the world.

Companies' efforts to trace their supply chains also represent real opportunities to address human trafficking and modern slavery. At Humanity United, we believe business and markets can be instrumental partners in advancing human freedom. Corporations, with their worldwide reach and deep engagement with labor—either directly or indirectly through their contractors and subcontractors—have the opportunity to ensure that severe exploitation is eliminated in all their operations, from the assembly of their products to the sourcing of raw materials. Increasingly, members of the business community are recognizing that they have not only the opportunity but also the responsibility to stop trafficking and modern day slavery.

Consumers and investors worldwide are also increasingly expecting them to exercise that responsibility.

We also need to recognize, however, that this work is not easy. Much of the most severe exploitation occurs at the very bottom of the supply chain. Whether it is the charcoal mined with slave labor that is used to make the pig iron to build the automobiles we drive, or in the palm oil contained in our toothpaste, forced labor can taint products we use every day. But more and more tools are being developed, from both the private and social sectors, for companies to help assess and remedy worker abuses deep in their supply chains. Companies around the world are slowly recognizing that there are not only ethical but also business reasons to clean up their supply chains. Whether it is to decrease disruptions that may occur when raw materials are extracted with forced labor, to improve conditions to maintain a workforce with lower costs for training, to win over talented employees who prefer to work for companies that avoid modern slavery, or to avoid damage to their brand, companies are increasingly examining their practices in both their facilities and their distant supply chains.

And laws like the California Transparency in Supply Chains Act are requiring them to report on what they are doing. The Congress should follow suit and make reporting on supply chains a national requirement. The Government of the United Kingdom is in the process of adopting such requirements for U.K. companies, and other G20 countries such as Australia and Canada may follow suit. The United States should help lead and coordinate this process not just for the sake of transparent supply chains, but so businesses can follow similar requirements around the world and not a patchwork of competing efforts and standards.

It is important to recognize that this work is not easy, and complete transparency for all levels in the supply chain is in most cases unreachable today. However, corporations can identify risks in their supply chains and delve deep to determine whether they have slavery in those areas with greatest risks. It is a calculation they make all the time.

We in civil society can help. The award-winning Coalition of Immokalee Workers has shown how corporations and growers can collaborate with workers to eliminate human trafficking and modern slavery and sexual abuse from the tomato fields of Florida. And Verité and Palantir Technologies are partnering to pilot a potentially transformative analytical product that will enable companies to unravel complex labor supply chains and identify risks of human trafficking and forced labor within them. Working closely with participating companies, Verité and Palantir will integrate corporate supply chain data, targeted field research on recruitment patterns and networks, and pertinent public information into a database platform. Verité experts will analyze the integrated data to illuminate particular labor supply networks and flag specific risks connected to one or multiple companies' supply chains. This data, augmented by Verité's high-quality analysis and targeted recommendations, will be pushed to web-based applications in Palantir that provide companies valuable information and actionable intelligence.

However, we in civil society should also recognize that a ''no tolerance policy'' does not mean ''slave free.'' We should work with companies to ensure that they take steps to address the problems they do discover, without pulling out altogether when a situation arises, which could hurt the workers whose condition we all want to see improve.

DEVELOPING UNLIKELY PARTNERSHIPS

Civil society can work across sectors and with companies in other ways to manage risks in its supply chains. For example, for many years the private sector and civil society have worked together in partnership on the challenges presented by clearing rainforest in Malaysia and Indonesia to create palm oil plantations. Palm oil is used in a variety of consumer products from soaps and shampoos to crackers and cookies. For a long time, the focus has been on the environment and loss of habitat for endangered species. Even today, many focus on this aspect of palm oil. The recent winner of a video competition for teens was a young woman worried that palm oil plantations would kill orangutans.[7] Yet she could have equally talked about the migrant workers who were forced to clear the rain forest and harvest palm for little or no pay and in horrific conditions. Civil society and major companies are working to move away from these silos toward a more holistic approach to sustainability, broadening guidelines to include labor protections that will meet the stated commitment by the Roundtable on Sustainable Palm Oil to prevent labor exploitation as well as environmental degradation. Indeed, the first fruits of this work came to light last week when Wilmar International, the largest palm oil producer in the world, established an online platform to promote transparency in its supply chain in partnership with Forest Trust.[8] Reporting required by economic, social, and governance reporting, and the transparency legislation I described above is also contributing to this increasing openness.

Similarly, Mr. Chairman, Humanity United is working with brick kiln owners in Nepal to provide incentives to reduce their emissions and to eliminate child and forced labor. However, we must always be careful about the unintended consequences of our action. Eliminating child labor in a particular brick kiln does not mean the child who is no longer enslaved is free: returning to his or her village, the child may be coerced into another setting with even worse conditions. As we take steps to free men, women, and children, we must make sure that we also take steps to break the chain of coercion by providing educational opportunities or providing alternatives for livelihood. These can often be small investments, but can make our efforts to free slaves sustainable. These risks are also why having baseline measurements and strong monitoring and evaluation are critical to ensure that interventions are actually reducing human trafficking and modern slavery.

Civil society also needs to work together more closely. In this connection, Humanity United brought together the Alliance to End Slavery and Trafficking. This coalition has grown to 14 leading human rights organizations, which focus on a range of issues from cooperation with law enforcement to assisting survivors to preventing trafficking in the first place. Focusing on legislative reforms, appropriations advocacy, and implementation by the executive branch, ATEST has helped sparked new initiatives across the human trafficking field. We have sought to press USAID, the Department of Labor, and the State Department to engage in rigorous monitoring and evaluation to find sustainable solutions to human trafficking and modern slavery, including establishing baselines and measuring impact. ATEST also seeks to further elevate the voices of survivors and help advance the broader U.S. movement by building deeper and wider networks and networks of networks to combat trafficking.

The faith community also has an enormous role to play and many are reaffirming a commitment to ending this terrible human rights abuse. Last Spring, Pope Francis met with trafficking survivors and in December hosted a convening of faith leaders to sign a declaration to abolish modern slavery by 2020. I hope that the Pope will further his efforts when he visits Washington later this year.

COLLABORATION AMONG DONORS AND PUBLIC-PRIVATE PARTNERSHIPS

One major challenge is the need for additional funding to combat human trafficking and modern slavery. The business of human trafficking is too large to allow fragmentation of efforts, which is why bringing government, business, and civil society together is key. But the private and public sector should also be better coordinated and mutually reinforcing.

In 2012, Humanity United and the Obama administration launched the Partnership for Freedom, a public-private partnership designed to bring private investment in innovation together with government experience to develop challenges to fight modern slavery. The first competition to improve support infrastructure for survivors of modern slavery concluded last year, with winners focused on innovative solutions to victim identification, health care, and shelter. However, a raft of additional innovative solutions were surfaced that we hope will get consideration from other donors. The second competition is being designed now.

Humanity United also partnered with the Legatum Foundation and the Walk Free Foundations, philanthropies based in the United Kingdom and Australia, respectively, to develop the Freedom Fund, a donor collaborative designed to mobilize the capital and knowledge needed to end modern slavery. The Freedom Fund has already launched targeted programs to tackle modern slavery in key countries and industries around the world.

In addition to donor partnerships, the private sector can also work directly with governments to combat human trafficking. Whether it is online marketplaces preventing their platform from being used for sex trafficking to companies providing needed data analysis, the corporate sector can play a major role working with law enforcement. The effort to stamp out Internet pornography by analyzing credit card data, for example, is a way that companies can work with civil society and law enforcement to further reduce sex trafficking in the future.

In this connection, Human Rights First, one of the Nation's leading human rights advocacy organizations, recently launched a campaign with a diverse set of actors across business, civil society, and the public sector to go after the business of human trafficking and modern slavery in all its forms, with the goal of decreasing the rewards and increasing the risks to perpetrators. I was privileged to participate in this launch, which included financial companies who showed how information they collect could help law enforcement here (with the Department of Justice) and abroad (with the Department of Treasury) to combat the scourge of modern slavery.

This shows the power of unlikely conversation to create social change. Humanity United's founders, Pierre and Pam Omidyar, are committed to a sustained effort to combat modern slavery. That's why they have made a second $50 million commitment to fight human trafficking and modern slavery. But they know they cannot win this fight alone, which is why Humanity United is committed to working to bring donors together, collaborating with the U.S. Government and building networks of civil society and survivors to make progress in the fight to end human trafficking and modern slavery.

CONCLUSION

Mr. Chairman, Senator Menendez and members of the committee, last week marked the end of National Slavery and Human Trafficking Prevention Month. Honorary months often seem to be a ritual of pronouncements and chest thumping, followed by little real action. Yet this year, it feels like we have reached a turning point in the fight to combat human trafficking. With multiple legislation passing the House and being introduced in the Senate, and the administration committed to cleaning its own supply chains, the tide may be turning against the perpetrators of this terrible human rights scourge.

Mr. Chairman, last week also marked the 150th year since the House of Representatives voted to approve the 13th Amendment, ending slavery in this great Nation. And this coming December, we will mark the adoption of the amendment as the law of the land. This committee can play an instrumental role in helping mark that anniversary by pushing forward the fight against human trafficking and modern slavery.

End Notes

[1] ILO, Profits and Poverty (2014).
[2] Id. See also ILO Global Estimate of Forced Labour (2012).
[3] http://www.ecpatusa.org/statistics.
[4] This number reflects both crisis calls by victims but also tips and other communications,http://www.polarisproject.org/resources/hotline-statistics.
[5] Zhang, S. X. (2012). Trafficking of Migrant Laborers in San Diego County: Looking for a Hidden Population. San Diego, CA: San Diego State University, https://www.ncjrs.gov/pdffiles1/nij/grants/240223.pdf.
[6] http://contratados.org.
[7] http://www.teensdream.net/(accessed February 2, 2015).
[8] http://www.triplepundit.com/2015/01/palm-oil-giant-launches-web-portal-make-supply-chain-transparent/.

The CHAIRMAN. Well, thank you for your testimony, and your entire statement will be made a part of the record. And thank you each for what you have said today and for sharing your experiences.

Mr. Kofi Annan, how aware are the people of Ghana that this slavery issue exists, and what is it that would motivate parents to allow their children to become a part of this?

Mr. ANNAN. Thank you very much. There have been a number of initiatives to create awareness, but there is a long way for us to go. We have a largely illiterate population, and, therefore, the platform to use for awareness is very important. If you use the mass media, you are targeting the elite, and they would have the information. But they are not the ones that are primarily affected by this issue, which means that in order to be effective in creating awareness in the various communities, you need to target them either in their own languages or in their communities. And that is where the gap is.

If we are supposed to get into every community with the message, then it means that the government must take leadership because government has access to almost all the media platforms, including the modern media and then the traditional media. And so, government must take the lead in all of this that we are doing. I believe that in the next few years, we need to at least reach half of the population. Now we do not even—we cannot see that even 20 percent of the population have been reached with the message. So that makes it very difficult for us to even assess ourselves as to how we are bringing everybody on board to create awareness of this situation.

The CHAIRMAN. And the parents, though they are obviously aware in many of the cases that their children are being victims of slavery, are they not?

Mr. ANNAN. In most cases when parents are selling their children, they are oblivious to what the children are going into because in most cases, they think that because they are poor, because they cannot take care of them, they are giving them up for the children to have a better life. They are going to have education. They are going to be taken care of better than they are being taken care of in their own homes. They are going to have better medical care, et cetera, et cetera.

So, they give these children out with all good intentions in most cases only for those children to end up being enslaved. And that is where the problem is, and that is where as soon as they get to know that the reason why they give the children out is different from how the children are being used, then they demand that the children to be returned. But because they do not have the capacity to go and bring their own children back, that is why they come to some of us to rescue the children for them. But we are not the ones they should come to. They ought to go to the government. This is where we will need to sustain and build upon the successes that we have started by creating more awareness, so the parents know that it is not a good place to send their children.

But the only way they should sustain their family and their children should be, you know, by having their children in a classroom, because wherever else they go, it ends up being a bad situation for them.

The CHAIRMAN. Thank you very much. Ms. Woworuntu, you are obviously incredibly well educated, had a great job in Indonesia, and yet ended up in a situation here in the United States through a recruiter where you were in obviously a very terrible situation, fortunately escaped, and are helping others. Could you tell me a little bit about how that occurred, what the experience was with the recruiter? And then post that, how the prosecution worked with you here in the United States?

Ms. WOWORUNTU. Thank you. At the moment, it was very hard in Indonesia due to the political and religious circumstances. The recruiters posted job applications in many media and newspapers saying that there is a certain job in the United States or other countries. There was a requirement to pay—in my case it was $3,000 U.S.—and the job was to work in the hotel, in the hospital or in some other jobs. So we see the applications with the promise of a big amount of salary, like $5,000 per month U.S. of work.

I worked as a manager in a bank. I could save only about $200. I felt the United States is the dreamland. The U.S. dollar was a big money for us, so why not? So I tried. I got the legitimate papers and I applied for the visa, and I got my visa, and flew to New York. During the prosecution, it was really hard for me because at that moment I was homeless. They did not give me a place to stay. When I cooperated with law enforcement, I was homeless for weeks and months, but they did not help me to stay in the shelter. And the law enforcement, they did not believe trafficking happens here.

The police let me down many times, but I kept trying so that one day they would listen to me. I went to different places to tell this story, but still they did not listen. And then a U.S. Navy officer listened to me at the place where I begged for food to eat. So he connected me to the FBI, and the FBI appointed one of the local precincts in New York to take my case.

But during the investigation, they thought I was—I am sorry in my language, they thought I was a sex worker. But I told them I had all of the copies of my passport. I flew to New York City with legal paperwork all complete. So they put me in the cold room without any food or drink. I asked them, I need to drink, I need to go to the bathroom, but they did not listen. They did not help me to handle my trauma in the investigation process. They just thought maybe I could cooperate, but I told them the truth. I told them what needed to be done.

The girls were there. The traffickers were there. I had all the addresses of the brothel and the hotels because I wrote it in a notebook. They did not believe me for a couple of hours, and then finally they said, okay. So we went to the brothel where I had worked, and my story was true, so they believed me.

So we rescued girls and put my trafficker into the justice system. I would testify, and we prosecuted—or they prosecuted, not me—three traffickers and some of the abusers because I was trafficked by organized crime. But I was not really happy because they threatened my family in Indonesia, and the government—the U.S. Government—went to the U.S. Embassy in Indonesia, got all of my paperwork, but they did not have a protection for my family.

The traffickers came to my family until 2007. It was about 6, 7 years after I escaped. My family also suffered. I got protection in the United States, but my family did not get it. So my trafficker are in Indonesia, and also the biggest travel agent in Indonesia, and the government did not do anything to them. That is what I propose if the U.S. Government were able to lead the connection or collaboration with all of different countries, not only Indonesia, to do this. Thank you.

The CHAIRMAN. Very impactful. Thank you both. And in order to be courteous to my colleagues, I will press on. I may want to come back, if it all right, and ask you a question.

Senator Menendez.

Senator MENENDEZ. Thank you, Mr. Chairman, and thank both of you for being willing to come forth and talk about your incredibly compelling experiences and the strength of human dignity to overcome. And it is really, I think, two very compelling stories among many I am sure that exists. I appreciate that, and I want to ask you questions in a minute.

Before I get to you, I want to ask Mr. Abramowitz, since the Trafficking Victims Protection Act was enacted in 2000, what has been the U.S. Government's top achievements for combating human trafficking, and what has been its key failures?

Mr. ABRAMOWITZ. Thanks for that question, Senator Menendez. I think that the first piece of it is they took an international agreement, the Palermo Protocol, which the United States became a party to, and they were actually able to try to take steps in other countries to implement it. I think as many of you know, international agreements and treaties like this, they get signed by countries, and then the countries do not take them seriously. They do not really try to implement Palermo Protocol. And through the Trafficking Office, the State Department was able to get countries around the world to pass laws, which as Mr. Haugen said in the first panel, really are pretty good. There are gaps. There are problems. And so then, the question became implementation. So the first, I think, achievement was that they really have got these issues mainstreamed into so many of these different places.

Second, I think the TIP Report then measures the behavior of these states, and has allowed civil society in these various countries to hold up this report, as much as some of the governments really hate that they do that, and say, look, here are the problems that you have. If you do not have these problems, explain it to the United States. Explain it to us. So it has really supported civil society in moving forward.

In terms of the challenges that the government has had, I think one of the major challenges is trying to position this issue within all the other challenges that the U.S. Government faces in relation with other countries. As I was saying, I am very concerned about the TIP Report this year without a TIP ambassador in place because there are pressures that come from the field to say, look, you know, this is a very important country. We are in the middle of negotiations on the trafficking report. Arguments about whether we cannot talk about Malaysian electronics, for example, is one issue that the U.S. Government was wrestling with over the last year.

I think trying to strengthen those efforts to try to have this be an important value within the U.S. Government is really critical. I also think this committee can really play a role by as witnesses come up to the committee, ask them about these issues, show them your importance when the ambassador nominees come through your office, talk to them about this issue, indicate that this is an important issue for all the members. I think that can really make a difference. Thank you.

Senator MENENDEZ. One other question. We heard a lot of the testimony so far about these recruiters, and they seem to be a significant part of the process in which people ultimately get led to trafficking because they create the nexus between the workforce and then the exploitation.

I get a sense that we do not really do very much about pursuing recruiters. Is there not a better way to go after these recruiters, to think about whether or not they should, as we find recruiters that are actually in the midst of the exploitation, deny them visas to the United States, take other actions, look at that as a criminal enterprise? Give me some sense about that.

Mr. ABRAMOWITZ. Yes. I think there are a number of different pieces that people are thinking about working on. Ed Royce's FORTE Act, which was mentioned, creates more transparency, but also creates a regulatory system which could be challenging in the current environment, that says that if you are going to be a recruiter, you have to register. And companies, if they use recruiters that are registered are safe if it turns out that it is a bad recruiter. But at least we will know who they are, and we can target our investigations, and that is a big problem around the world.

In Nepal, which is going to send 900,000 to 1.5 million workers to the gulf and to Qatar as part of the World Cup infrastructure, there are 80,000 unregistered individuals who are recruiting these people from villages all over the country. So I think we have to try to talk to the source countries and try to get that under control.

One of the things that some countries are trying is to say is, no recruitment fees at all. If it turns out that the worker can show that there were recruitment fees paid, then that worker can go to the company who is using that labor and ask for reimbursement. If the companies are on the hook for having to pay recruitment fees, they are going to start making sure that the recruiters are not doing anything that is illegal, and I think that is a reform that Qatar is looking at, for example. They have not quite implemented it yet. They said they were going to do some of things. They have not done them yet. But I think some of those kinds of those kinds of reforms can really help.

Senator MENENDEZ. Okay. You mentioned Nepal. The Guardian reported that in 2014, Nepal citizens working in Qatar, that one died every 2 days because of extreme heat and conditions that should not be accepted. So I think we have the Qatari Foreign Minister here. It might be a good opportunity to raise some of these issues with him.

Mr. ABRAMOWITZ. I agree.

Senator MENENDEZ. Ms. Woworuntu, first of all, thank you for your work that you are doing in the State of New Jersey on the Human Trafficking Commission. We appreciate your service. And in that regard, you know, when you talked about your experience, how is we—that you think from your experience, that we get law enforcement and the judicial system to work better with trafficking victims to investigate and successfully prosecute those who put you into slavery?

You described a set of circumstances in which you were not believed. You were thought to be a voluntary sex worker. A whole different set of circumstances, and you almost had to fight for credibility. It almost seems to me that there should be some type of basis under which you are believed until proven that that is not true. I mean, give me a sense of how you think we might be able to do better.

Ms. WOWORUNTU. In 2014, I was with some other survivors at the Federal level, at a survivor's hearing at the White House. So I gave my voice that something needs to be done about how law enforcement works with victims of human trafficking. I used ''victim'' because they need to get help. They need to get services. They need to be listened to.

So, I talked to the law enforcement at the Department of Justice and OVC and said that, one, they need to better identify the victims of human trafficking in sex and labor, because to identify both sex and labor victims they need to have specific understanding that there are differences. Identifying sex trafficking can be hard for law enforcement because they will not tell you if they are victims because they are afraid.

For example, young girls are trafficked and then the law enforcement—excuse my language—busted the place and pulled the girls to the prison and treated them as criminal, not as a victim, especially under 18. These are victims, children, yes, 18 years old, children, girls that have become victims. But our law enforcement still treats them as criminals. They are not in prostitution. They are victims. So somehow the law enforcement who work directly in the field, they did not know. They lack understanding of how they should treat the victims.

Second, they need sensitivity training to identify the victims of human trafficking. Sensitivity training should include cultural— American culture and Indonesian culture, Chinese culture, are different, so they need to understand how to deal with certain people who came from around the world, and with the domestic victim as well.

And then the third thing is having the organizations who give direct victims' services involved in the investigation so the investigation will be done properly with the right time management, and also have case management. Usually law enforcement did not work with case and time management in how to identify the victims, or how to solve the problem.

Senator MENENDEZ. Thank you. Thank you both for your insights, and I just want to know, Ms. Woworuntu, that by New Jersey standards, "busted" is a mild world. [Laughter.]

So, thank you.

Ms. WOWORUNTU. Thank you.

The CHAIRMAN. There is more I could say, but I will not. [Laughter.]

The CHAIRMAN. Senator Kaine.

Senator KAINE. Thank you, Mr. Chairman, and thank you to you all for your very illuminating testimony, and to the chair and ranking member for calling this hearing. The timing is exquisite. Yesterday the Vatican announced that this Sunday would be an international day of prayer against human trafficking, and the date of February 8 was chosen because it is the feast day for St. Josephine Bakhita, who was born in 1868 in Darfur, kidnapped at age 9, and then sold into slavery twice in her life, once in Sudan and once in Italy, before she passed away in 1947. And so, that is a good thing. I think the church communities around the world, and this is an ecumenical effort, educating us all about signs and what we can do to help is very important.

I just have sort of one question, and I am not exactly sure—in some ways I had a State Department person here, but let me just throw the question out. And, Ms. Woworuntu, it is kind of about your experience. Trafficking in slavery, different kinds. There is between nations other than the United States. There is slavery and trafficking within the United States. Your story is one from another nation into the United States, and I want to ask about that.

It would seem that we should be able to develop training for consular officials who are interviewing applicants for visas. We should be able to develop training for our Customs and Border Patrol folks that are interviewing visitors as they come into the United States, that would not always discover whether somebody was a victim of trafficking, but would, you know—there has got to be some warning signs that we should be training our people about.

Is that something that we do well already, or is there more we can do with our consular officials and our Border Patrol folks to make sure that we can stop trafficking as it is occurring? And I would love to hear from any of you on that.

Ms. WOWORUNTU. Yes. The authorization mentioned about how Department of State will work on trafficking prevention through using awareness videos in all U.S. embassies around the world. But the work is not perfect, and we need to work more. Right now, Homeland Security has a pamphlet. Department of Transportation, also UNICEF, has pamphlets everywhere raising awareness. And the most important is for embassies around the world to have information about the rights of the persons who would want to enter to another country.

So far, there is not much information given about the rights accorded to visitors. I am really advocating about the prevention in the Department of State, and I will diligently work for that.

Senator KAINE. Excellent. Mr. Abramowitz.

Mr. ABRAMOWITZ. Senator Kaine, I think this is a very important issue. As Ms. Woworuntu was just saying, in the 2008 act, we required that there be this pamphlet that is given out to every worker, and the 2013 act required that this video be actually put in place. And I think those are good things to try to protect the worker who is coming to the United States so they know who to call. There are all these stories about how the worker held onto this little pamphlet and stuck it in their shoe, and finally when they had an opportunity, they were able to call a hotline and get out of their slavery.

I think the problem for the consular officer is that, as in Ms. Wororuntu's case, the case presents reasonably well. There is an application. There is a job that is supposedly there and so on, and then they have a very short amount of time to review. I think that there could be a better way of trying to determine whether a real job is really happening there, and also trying to find out who are the bad labor recruiters.

Take her case. This was a major labor recruiting firm that brought her into this situation, so they should be able to go to the recruiters and say, what is going on here, we have problem cases coming from you, and work with the government to try to say you have got to work on these cases. We have very skilled Foreign Service nationals in our embassies in the consular section, and if we devoted more resources to doing more investigations of which of these labor recruiting companies were really a problem, that could make a big difference.

Senator KAINE. Like the other members of the committee, I do a good bit of traveling. And any time I travel, I try to sit down with our troops who are in the places I am, but I also try to sit down with Foreign Service officers on their first or second tours just to hear about the challenges. And almost all in early tours are working in consular capacities, and, you know, I am struck by how hard their job is. The volume of applications is huge, and it is very difficult.

But it would seem like, you know, we ought to be able to give kind of almost profile information. You know, here is the kind of thing to watch out for that might suggest that there is trafficking going on. And we ought to have enough institutional expertise within State, and DHS, and everybody that is—DOL and DOJ that is working on this, to give that kind of information, both in the consular officers and at the Border Patrol sites. So that is a question that I will follow up with maybe for the record or follow up directly with the agencies about.

Mr. ABRAMOWITZ. Yes, I think that between the visa fraud section at State, the Department of Homeland Security, and the Justice Department, you could put together an interesting profile, of course, context by context.

Senator KAINE. Yes.

Mr. ABRAMOWITZ. I will say in the earlier panel, Senator Kaine, you missed an exchange about diplomatic visas, and there are some real concerns around whether the Protocol Bureau and the State Department is doing enough. You all are familiar with the Khobragade case where there was a case brought against an Indian diplomat in New York because of forced labor with a domestic servant, and because of a variety of issues that case was let go.

And as Ms. Bader-Blau mentioned in the previous panel, there are these questions about what is going on with India and whether they are trying to get out of the oversight framework that was created in the 2008 act over a specific visa category that is usually used to go to a different visa category for these domestic servants. And I do think that that should be looked at by you and the staff to see what is going on there. Thank you.

Senator KAINE. All right. Thank you very much for your testimony today. Thank you, Mr. Chairman.

The CHAIRMAN. Thank you, Senator Kaine. I want to thank you for being here. I think this has been most impactful. I want to thank our ranking member for his shared interest in this topic and for allowing this hearing to go forward today as it has, and hopefully it will produce results here.

To the two witnesses who have been victims, I want to thank you for the courage to be here, but also taking your experiences and using it to help other people, and to help us today, first, to understand some of the cultural issues and the lack of awareness. I mean, it seems to me that one of the easy to produce outcomes is to make sure people are more fully aware, and that parents understand what is happening in various countries with their young ones.

And to understand the tremendous plight of victims, who, in many cases, are not dealt with as victims. That is an experience that we heard from others. And, again, just creating more awareness with the law enforcement agencies, but also making sure that we use best practices, and your efforts to work through public policy to deal with this effectively. All three of you have been outstanding witnesses. Our first panel certainly was a very good panel. And as Senator Kaine mentioned, I cannot imagine a better time for us to be focused on this.

The issue regarding foreign officials, we do have a meeting today with a Foreign Minister, and, candidly, the topic is ISIS. And a lot of times we do get caught up, as we should, in important issues of national security. But to be aware of this issue also, and to be able to push this as we meet with other officials, but also to produce some public policy hopefully that will deal with this on a far grander scale with a much bigger vision.

So thank you all for being here. Your testimony was outstanding.

And for the information of the members, the record will remain open until the close of business on Friday, February the 6th, including for members to submit questions for the record. We ask, if you will, to respond as promptly as you can to those. Your responses will also be made a part of the record.

And with the thanks of the committee, this hearing is now adjourned. Thank you.

Mr. ABRAMOWITZ. Thank you, Mr. Chairman.

Ms. WOWORUNTU. Thank you.

The CHAIRMAN. Thank you.

[Whereupon, at 11:50 a.m., the hearing was adjourned.]

ADDITIONAL MATERIAL SUBMITTED FOR THE RECORD

SUBMITTED FOR THE RECORD BY DAVID ABRAMOWITZ

[From The Hill (Capitol Hill Publishing Corp.), Jan. 30, 2015]

MOMENTUM FOR ANTI-TRAFFICKING BUILDS, BUT AMBASSADORSHIP STILL VACANT

(By David Abramowitz, contributor)

This week marks the end of National Slavery and Human Trafficking Prevention Month. Honorary months often seem to be a ritual of pronouncements and chest thumping, followed by little real action. Yet this year, it feels like we have reached a turning point in the fight to combat human trafficking.

Fifteen years ago, human trafficking was a niche issue with only a few Members of the U.S. Congress paying attention. In the last few years, however, the circle of champions has exploded. Just this week, 12 pieces of legislation were considered on the House floor touching a wide range of issues, from child welfare to increasing the U.S. Government's focus on trafficking to finding more resources for survivors. The Senate is also gearing up to move forward with its own bipartisan proposals (including the Runaway and Homeless Youth and Trafficking Prevention Act), and the Obama administration has just released long-awaited regulations to implement the President's Executive order to prevent human trafficking in federal procurement.

Civil society engagement in the field has also continued to grow. Human Rights First (HRF), a leader in human rights advocacy, is launching a new campaign to disrupt the business of human trafficking which will focus on more prosecutions of all perpetrators, promoting a victim-centered approach and pushing the U.S. Government and businesses to do more to prevent and respond to modern slavery. (Full disclosure: I have been working with HRF to shape this new campaign.) Furthermore, philanthropic partnerships like the Freedom Fund (which Humanity United supports) are bringing further coordination and new funding to this field, both here and abroad.

The faith community is also reaffirming a commitment to ending this terrible human rights abuse. Last spring, Pope Francis met with trafficking survivors and in December hosted a convening of faith leaders to sign a declaration to abolish modern slavery by 2020.

With all this activity however, there is one glaring gap: the lack of an Ambassador at Large to Monitor and Combat Trafficking in Persons. The so-called TIP ambassador position at the U.S. State Department has been vacant for 2 months, with even longer delays ahead given that the position requires Senate confirmation. The U.S. is considered one of the global leaders in combating human trafficking and the absence of the TIP ambassador can jeopardize U.S. leadership.

Finding the right candidate is challenging. The TIP ambassador will need to help build this field and heal the remaining fissures that exist within it. Such a person must be committed to an inclusive and balanced approach to combat labor and sex trafficking of both adults and children. The ambassador will also have to be committed to improving services for survivors. Additionally, an individual who can focus on prevention of trafficking beyond deterrence could have a major impact on the field. And, of course, the ambassador must be able to produce a strong annual Trafficking in Persons Report. The TIP report is one of the key tools for asserting U.S. global leadership in this space. Foreign governments may complain about their treatment in the report, but they respond when called out in this public manner. Given the diverse interests involved in combating human trafficking, this diplomat will have to work across stakeholder communities, foreign governments, with the business community and even within the U.S. Government so that the TIP Report, the TIP office and thus U.S. efforts to combat trafficking are as strong as possible.

With so much ambition and enthusiasm around the fight to end human trafficking and modern slavery, we need an ambassador who can take this momentum and harness it. She or he must steer it toward meaningful, practical change for all victims of modern slavery suffering in terrible conditions; for survivors who are seeking to overcome their exploitation; for businesses with complex supply chains; and for governments seeking to address (or willfully ignore) the current manifestations of slavery within their borders.

The gains of the past 15 years are starting to bear fruit. Now is the time for action and sustainable solutions—and a new TIP ambassador can play an important role in bringing those solutions to reality.

ENDING MODERN DAY SLAVERY: THE ROLE OF U.S. LEADERSHIP

WEDNESDAY, FEBRUARY 11, 2015

U.S. SENATE,
COMMITTEE ON FOREIGN RELATIONS,
Washington, DC.

The committee met, pursuant to notice, at 2:18 p.m., in room SD–419, Dirksen Senate Office Building, Hon. Bob Corker (chairman of the committee) presiding.

Present: Senators Corker, Johnson, Gardner, Menendez, Cardin, and Shaheen.

OPENING STATEMENT OF HON. BOB CORKER, U.S. SENATOR FROM TENNESSEE

The CHAIRMAN. This hearing of the Senate Foreign Relations Committee will come to order.

And thank you so much for being here. I will introduce you in one moment.

I want to thank the other committee members for their interest.

We have convened this hearing to understand how U.S. leadership can best be deployed to deal a mortal wound to modern slavery. Last week, the committee heard from two panels of private witnesses. We received testimony from leaders in the effort to combat modern slavery. We also heard from brave individuals who escaped from modern slavery and went on to help others.

Today we welcome Dr. Sarah Sewall. I have heard many good things about the Under Secretary of State for Civilian Security, Democracy, and Human Rights at the U.S. Department of State. The State Department's office to monitor and combat trafficking in persons falls under your purview, and we appreciate your efforts.

Conflict exposes vulnerable people, especially women and children, to being enslaved and exploited. The horrifying examples set by ISIL and Boko Haram could not be starker.

But even in countries with laws and institutions, insidious forms of modern slavery exists. Perversely labor recruiters extract money from impoverished people with empty promises and deliver them into bondage and sexual exploitation.

For 14 years, as defined and authorized by Congress, the State Department has issued an annual report on trafficking in persons. This report, as Secretary Kerry has said, sets the gold standard. The report reviews the efforts of countries to address trafficking in persons especially in the most severe forms. Its findings are not always welcome, but we know they have made a difference.

Under Secretary Sewall has said that almost every issue she touches has implications for human trafficking. Whether working with the Bureau of Counterterrorism, Democracy, Human Rights, and Labor, Population Migration and Refugees, International Narcotics and Law Enforcement Affairs, Conflict and Stabilization Operations, often there is a trafficking angle.

Today we hope to learn how U.S. leadership is already making a difference and how, working in partnership with the State Department and reaching out to like-minded governments, we can take our efforts to the next level to find the best way forward to begin the process in earnest of putting an end to modern slavery. Thank you.

And with that, I will turn to our distinguished ranking member, Bob Menendez.

OPENING STATEMENT OF HON. ROBERT MENENDEZ, U.S. SENATOR FROM NEW JERSEY

Senator MENENDEZ. Thank you, Mr. Chairman, and thank you for your focus on addressing the issue of trafficking in all of its forms. Sexual exploitation, forced labor, forced marriage, debt bondage, and the sale and exploitation of children around the world should be a global cry for justice. But as Benjamin Franklin said, justice will not be served until those of us who are unaffected are as outraged as those who are.

Today we are all outraged at the violence, psychological terror, the greed that drives human trafficking. We are outraged that there are 50 million refugees and displaced people around the world, the largest number since World War II, many of whom are targets of traffickers. We are outraged that there are 21 million victims of human trafficking, over 5 million of whom are children, and that forced labor generates about $150-plus billion in profits annually, the second-largest income source for international criminals next to the drug trade.

We know that NGOs and civil society have been doing what they can to combat this scourge, but we can all do more. The State Department's Office of Trafficking in Persons has been nothing less than extraordinary, but it remains understaffed, underresourced and without leadership, leaving Under Secretary Sewall's efforts all the more important. Certainly Government can do better. Companies can do more. They can clean up the supply chains and make that information public. The public can be more aware of who picks the fruit on their breakfast cereal in the morning, how many women and children it took trapped in a sweat shop to sew the dresses and shirts they are wearing.

In my view, reform of the labor recruitment process and the regulation of labor recruiters is crucial to helping enslaved Bangladeshi women serving as domestic servants in the Middle East, construction workers from Nepal building World Cup Soccer stadiums in Qatar, or Rohingya men trapped on Thai shrimp boats supplying American fish markets. Those are just some of those elements.

And finally, Mr. Chairman, let me just say I am also outraged at the scourge of diplomats who themselves are trafficking domestic workers, bringing them to the United States to work in embassies and missions here in Washington and around the world. We had a case like this in my home State of New Jersey. I know Secretary Kerry has committed to preventing such abuse, and I look forward to hearing what is actually being done. And I am anxious to hear what is being done to mitigate the diplomatic situation that arose in the high-profile case of an Indian Deputy Counsel General in New York who was charged with visa fraud in a trafficking-like situation. But I look forward to seeing what we are doing in that regard as well, and I look forward to hearing our witness.

The CHAIRMAN. Thank you, Senator Menendez, and thank you for your shared interest in this issue and your comments.

And now we will turn to our witness. Our witness today is Dr. Sarah Sewall, the Under Secretary of State for Civilian Security, Democracy, and Human Rights. She was sworn in as Under Secretary on February 20, 2014, and serves concurrently as the Special Coordinator for Tibetan Issues.

Over the previous decade, Dr. Sewall taught at Harvard Kennedy School of Government, where she also served as director of the Carr Center for Human Rights Policy, launched the MARO Project, Mass Atrocities Response Operations. In 2012, she was Minerva Chair at the Naval War College. During the Clinton administration, Dr. Sewall served as the inaugural Deputy Assistant Secretary of Defense for Peacekeeping and Humanitarian Assistance. Prior to joining the executive branch, she served 6 years as the senior foreign policy advisor to U.S. Senate Majority Leader George Mitchell.

I want to thank you for being here. You have had a very distinguished career. You are either really, really qualified or cannot keep a job. [Laughter.]

But you have done a lot of different things. But I think it is the first.

Thank you for being here and sharing your testimony. And we will remind you that your full statement will be entered into the record. Thank you.

STATEMENT OF HON. SARAH SEWALL, UNDER SECRETARY OF STATE FOR CIVILIAN SECURITY, DEMOCRACY, AND HUMAN RIGHTS, U.S. DEPARTMENT OF STATE, WASHINGTON, DC

Dr. SEWALL. Thank you very much, Chairman Corker, Senator Menendez, members of the committee, ladies and gentlemen.

It is a pleasure to be here today, and I want to begin by thanking you and many members of this committee for their leadership in combating trafficking in persons. And on behalf of the State Department, I look forward to working closely with you to tackle this terrible crime and human rights abuse.

I think it is fair to say that trafficking in persons and the efforts to combat it is a personal priority of the Secretary. It is certainly a personal priority of mine, and it is a priority for the State Department and this administration. It harms people and communities. It corrupts labor markets and global supply chains. It undermines the rule of law and stability.

And in today's global community, we are all as citizens and as consumers impacted by slavery even if we do not realize it. I recently took a survey on SlaveryFootprint.org, and it was a stark reminder that many of the products I use on a daily basis, the battery in my cell phone, the chocolate that I eat, the cotton clothes that I wear may have been produced by slaves. Slavery Footprint has reached millions of consumers globally, giving them a voice to demand that the products they buy are made free of forced labor. It is seed-funded by the State Department, therefore one example of the types of programs that we are supporting to elevate the global conversation on modern slavery.

The U.S. Government is making major efforts here at home to combat this scourge. As the largest purchaser of goods and services in the United States and overseas, the American Government must set the highest standards for its business practices. Executive Order 13627 was the President's Executive order committing to strengthening protections against human trafficking in Federal contracting. The Federal Acquisition Regulatory Council published updates to the Federal acquisition regulation implementing this order.

In addition, the State Department funded Verité, a labor rights NGO, to develop a range of tools and resources for Federal contractors and businesses to help them mitigate the risks of human trafficking in their supply chains.

We have come a long way, Mr. Chairman, in the last 15 years; 166 states are now party to the Palermo Protocol. Human trafficking has moved from a misunderstood side issue to an international priority. Over 100 countries have passed antitrafficking laws, and many have established specialized law enforcement units, victim assistance mechanisms, and public awareness campaigns. But, of course, much work remains.

Although the ILO estimates that there are 21 million victims of forced labor around the world, the State Department's Trafficking in Persons TIP Report notes that fewer than 45,000 trafficking victims had been identified by governments in the year 2014. Convictions of traffickers remains woefully insufficient. Adequate antitrafficking laws are an important first step to address the troubling trend, but these laws must be enforced and traffickers held accountable. Aware and capable states are the key to tackling this crime, an issue to which I shall return.

Now, as you know, the TIP Report has been a critically important tool. The report assesses the adequacy of national laws in prohibiting and punishing trafficking, and it evaluates government actions to prosecute suspects and protect victims. The report's tier rankings help hold governments accountable in their efforts to develop the policies and structures to fight this crime. Researchers have documented the correlation between tier ranking downgrades and states' subsequent enactment of antitrafficking legislation.

The TIP Report makes specific recommendations for how each country can better prevent trafficking, prosecute suspected perpetrators, and assist victims. And these recommendations in turn guide U.S. diplomacy and they serve as a roadmap for institutional changes.

Additionally, the State Department and USAID combine antitrafficking and labor rights diplomacy with specific programming to help countries achieve better results. State's TIP Office currently oversees 98 projects worth over $59 million in 71 countries. And these projects target both sex and labor trafficking through implementation of what is known as the 3P paradigm, prevention, protection of victims, and prosecution of suspected traffickers.

Much of our antitrafficking assistance helps partner governments build their own capacity. So in the last 2 years, Botswana, Haiti, Maldives, Papua New Guinea, and Seychelles all passed antitrafficking laws. And last March, the Bahamas secured its first conviction.

Since 2001, USAID has programmed approximately $180 million in antitrafficking activities in 70 countries and regional missions. And in Jordan, USAID integrated countertrafficking activities into a broader human rights program in combating sexual- and gender-based violence, early marriage, and child labor among Syrian refugees and host communities.

In 2013, Congress saw fit to give the State Department a new innovative tool, the Child Protection Compacts. Through the partnership, we will develop tailored policies to focus on one particular case, and I am pleased to announce today that we have proposed our first partner in that CPC partnership, which is to work with the Government of Ghana.

The struggle against modern slavery is one of the interconnected threats and opportunities. It involves good governance, and the broader work of State and AID, in partnership with other actors, is just vital if we are to truly tackle this global challenge. Conflict, corruption, and underdevelopment fuel trafficking risks, and the U.S. Government works to address these underlying causes as part of our foreign policy, even as we have pioneered innovative programs specifically aimed against human slavery.

I am very proud, Mr. Chairman, of the leading role the United States has played with strong leadership from Congress in elevating the global profile of this issue, helping free individuals from modern slavery, and galvanizing the work of others. The road is long in our battle against human trafficking, but working with global partners, the United States will not relent in our multipronged approach to combat the crime.

We welcome Congress' interest. We welcome your interest particularly, Mr. Chairman, and we look forward to working together and to the dialogue. Thank you.

[The prepared statement of Dr. Sewall follows:]

PREPARED STATEMENT OF DR. SARAH SEWALL

Chairman Corker, Senator Menendez, members of the committee, ladies and gentlemen, thank you, Mr. Chairman and members of the committee, for your leadership in combating trafficking in persons. On behalf of the State Department, I look forward to working closely with you to tackle this terrible crime and human rights abuse. This issue is a policy priority for the administration and Secretary Kerry, in particular, and I thank you for the opportunity to speak today.

What do we, in the U.S. Government, mean when we talk about human trafficking? Under the Trafficking Victims Protection Act (or TVPA), trafficking in persons includes forced labor, forced prostitution of adults, and the prostitution of children. The term "human trafficking" describes acts of recruiting, harboring, transporting, providing, or obtaining a person for compelled labor or commercial sex acts through the use of force, fraud, or coercion, although inducing minors into the commercial sex trade is considered trafficking even if no force, fraud, or coercion is involved. It can include, but does not require, movement of individuals.

Trafficking in persons harms people and corrodes communities. It corrupts labor markets and global supply chains that are essential to a thriving global economy. It undermines rule of law and stability. Fighting trafficking in persons is the smart thing to do, and it is the right thing to do. As President Obama has said, "Our fight against human trafficking is one of the great human rights causes of our time, and the United States will continue to lead it.'' It is our responsibility as a country and as individuals to protect the universal values of liberty and freedom.

There is a lot that we as individuals can do to join this struggle against modern slavery. I recently went to SlaveryFootprint.org and took a survey to learn how my consumption habits are connected to modern-day slavery. It was a stark reminder—many of the products I use on a daily basis, the battery in my cell phone, the chocolate I eat, the cotton clothes I wear, may have been produced from the work of dozens of slaves. Slavery Footprint, a project seed-funded by the State Department, has reached millions of consumers globally and given them a voice to insist that the food we eat and the products we buy are made free of forced labor.

Let me begin by discussing what the U.S. Government is doing here at home. Federal agencies have been going the extra mile, spurred by President Obama's March 2012 direction to his Cabinet to redouble the administration's efforts to combat human trafficking. The President's Interagency Task Force to Monitor and Combat and Trafficking in Persons, which Congress established and Secretary Kerry currently chairs, has strengthened its collaborative work, including developing and implementing the Nation's first-ever ''Federal Strategic Action Plan on Services for Victims of Human Trafficking in the United States.'' Government agencies are enabling law enforcement and service providers to deploy resources more effectively and raising public awareness both at home and abroad.

Federal agencies are also working to expand partnerships with civil society and the private sector to bring more resources to bear in fighting this injustice. The Treasury Department's Financial Crimes Enforcement Network issued an advisory last September to financial institutions on recognizing ''red flags'' that may indicate financial activity related to human trafficking as well as the distinct crime of human smuggling. The advisory provides common terms that financial institutions may use when reporting activity related to these crimes that will assist law enforcement in better identifying possible cases of human trafficking.

As the largest single purchaser of goods and services both in the United States and around the world, the U.S. Government must set the highest standards for our own business practices. With Executive Order 13627, the President committed the Federal Government to strengthen protections against human trafficking in federal contracting. Just over a week ago, the Federal Acquisition Regulatory Council published updates to the Federal Acquisition Regulation, as required by this Executive order and related requirements in the Ending Trafficking in Government Contracting Act (set forth in the National Defense Authorization Act for 2013), establishing a number of new and important antitrafficking safeguards. In addition, the State Department funded Verité, an award-winning labor rights NGO, to develop a range of tools and resources for all businesses—not just federal contractors—committed to preventing trafficking. As part of this initiative, Verité just published a report entitled ''Strengthening Protections Against Trafficking in Persons in Federal and Corporate Supply Chains,'' which details the risks of human trafficking in 11 key sectors where federal procurement is significant. This type of supply chain risk analysis can help federal contractors, other businesses, and consumers identify and mitigate human trafficking.

Here in the United States, we have modern-day heroes who are changing how we do business. The members of the Coalition of Immokalee Workers have transformed Florida tomato fields from a place of widespread egregious exploitation into one where workers' rights are not only respected, but prioritized. They demanded that the large restaurant and supermarket chains purchase tomatoes at a fair price. On January 29, in front of leaders from the private sector, civil society, and the Federal Government assembled for a White House Forum on Combating Trafficking in Persons in Supply Chains, Secretary Kerry presented the Coalition with the 2015 Presidential Award for Extraordinary Efforts to Combat Trafficking in Persons. Among the accomplishments for which the Coalition was recognized is its Fair Foods Program, a highly successful worker-based social responsibility model that leverages the market power of major corporate buyers, coupled with strong consumer awareness, worker training, and robust enforcement mechanisms to end labor trafficking, enhance wages, and promote workplace rights.

Congress and the American people also have much to be proud of. This year marks the 15th anniversary of the Trafficking Victims Protection Act, as well as the United Nations Protocol to Prevent, Suppress, and Punish Trafficking in Persons, known as the Palermo Protocol. We have come a long way in the past 15 years: 166 States are now party to the Palermo Protocol. Human trafficking has moved from a misunderstood issue to an international priority. More than 100 countries have passed antitrafficking laws and many have established specialized law enforcement units, set up trafficking victim assistance mechanisms, and launched public awareness campaigns aimed at combating this worldwide crime that affects every country.

However, we have a long way to go. Although the International Labor Organization (ILO) estimates there are 21 million victims of forced labor around the world, the 2014 Trafficking in Persons (TIP) Report notes that fewer than 45,000 trafficking victims were identified in 2014. Convictions of traffickers remain woefully insufficient given the magnitude of the crime. This is a troubling trend we must continue working to address. Having adequate antitrafficking laws is an important first step for any country, but these laws must be enforced, and traffickers held accountable.

Fueled by the dedication of officers in every bureau of the Department as well as at U.S. missions around the world, the TVPA-mandated TIP Report plays an important role in confronting this lucrative crime. In accordance with the Minimum Standards of the TVPA, the TIP Report assesses the adequacy of national laws in prohibiting and punishing the crime and evaluates government actions to prosecute suspects and protect victims. Countries and territories are ranked by tiers based on these standards. Tier 1 countries fully comply with the Minimum Standards. Tier 2 and Tier 2 Watch List countries do not, but are making significant efforts to do so. Tier 3 countries are not making significant efforts to fully comply with the Minimum Standards. These rankings help hold governments accountable in their efforts to fight human trafficking. They motivate governments to develop policies and structures to fight this serious crime. In fact, researchers have documented the correlation between tier-ranking downgrades and states' subsequent enactment of antitrafficking legislation.

The TIP Report includes specific recommendations for how each country can better prevent this crime, prosecute its suspected perpetrators, and assist its victims. These recommendations are the heart of the report. They guide U.S. diplomacy and engagement on human trafficking issues—both publicly and privately. They also serve as a roadmap to better address the problem—not for the sake of improving a tier ranking, but to make institutional changes that will put additional traffickers behind bars, help victims get assistance, and prevent exploitation of the vulnerable.

A key element to the TIP Report is identifying and documenting trends in types of exploitation, in criminal strategies, and in raising awareness and cracking down on the crime. For example, over time we have seen more governments recognize the important contributions of NGOs in this fight and improved cooperation, especially in the areas of victim identification and victim services. Many countries are beginning to grapple with the extent and challenges of detecting forced labor. While we have seen an increase in the detection of forced labor cases, there is still a large disparity in government efforts to address forced labor, which is considered to be more prevalent globally than sex trafficking. In victim identification and services, women and girls appear to comprise the vast majority of identified victims of sex trafficking and are also a substantial portion of labor trafficking victims. In addition, we have seen links in regional and transregional human trafficking to economic disparity and migration flows, the presence of organized crime, conflicts and political instability, official corruption and weak rule of law.

The State Department and USAID have sought to combine antitrafficking and labor rights diplomacy with complementary programming to help countries achieve results. The State Department's Trafficking in Persons (TIP) Office is currently overseeing 98 projects worth over $59 million in 71 countries around the world. The TIP Office's foreign assistance targets both sex trafficking and labor trafficking through implementation of the "3P" paradigm of prevention, protection of victims, and prosecution of suspected traffickers. A fourth "P" for partnership, is also a critical element in the majority of programs. Along with funding NGOs that offer services to trafficking victims, much of our antitrafficking assistance is designed to help partner governments build their own capacity to fight human trafficking. In the last 2 years, Botswana, Haiti, Maldives, Papua New Guinea, and Seychelles all passed antitrafficking laws, and Morocco and Namibia have drafted antitrafficking legislation. In March 2014, the Bahamas secured its first conviction for human trafficking. Maldives also saw its first trafficking conviction.

Successful programs often work in close partnership with host country governments and key stakeholders to encourage a comprehensive response to trafficking. For example, in Afghanistan, a State Department grantee partnered with the Ministry of Women's Affairs to establish an advocacy council comprised of local nongovernmental organizations and relevant government agencies to enhance protection measures for victims of human trafficking. The council and government coalition partners have adopted minimum standards of care for trafficking victims and provide training and capacity-building assistance. The TIP Office is currently funding a global project that integrates survivors of trafficking into a 6-month vocational and educational program in the hotel service industry. The project provides survivors and at-risk youth with life skills and vocational training through a combination of training and practical instruction in coordination with leading hotels. This project has already demonstrated successes in Mexico and Vietnam and was recently expanded to India and Ethiopia.

Labor programming from the State Department's Bureau of Democracy, Human Rights, and Labor (DRL) targets forced labor through strengthening the organizational and technical capacity of worker rights organizations, providing socioeconomic support and alternative livelihood opportunities to exploited workers, and strengthening systems to promote identification and remediation of labor law violations in a variety of sectors at the local, regional, and international levels. DRL's grants are designed to bolster civil society and labor's capacity to play a role in migration policymaking. The Department makes an effort to ensure that trade and investment policies, agreements, and preference programs consistently address work conditions for both national and foreign migrant workers. In collaboration with the State Department's Economic Bureau and the Department of Commerce, DRL partners with multinational corporations, business councils, and American Chambers of Commerce to convey expectations on labor rights both to host governments and to companies within their supply chains.

The State Department's Bureau of Population, Refugees, and Migration funds eight regional migration programs that build government and civil society capacity to identify and protect vulnerable migrants, including victims of human trafficking. The Bureau also funds a program that facilitates the family reunification of foreign trafficking victims identified in the United States and contributes to a global fund that helps stranded trafficking victims voluntarily return home.

Corruption and an environment of impunity are significant factors contributing to the practice of human trafficking. The Bureau of International Narcotics and Law Enforcement Affairs has some of the Department's strongest tools for strengthening rule of law and helping governments prevent and combat corruption. Its anticorruption and law enforcement programming provides training to law enforcement officers and the judiciary on investigating human trafficking and corruption cases and address the linkages among human trafficking, corruption, and organized crime.

Interagency training at U.S. missions overseas, including Brazil, Cambodia, the Philippines, Togo, the Dominican Republic, and Hong Kong, will enable State Department, DHS, and FBI agents to pursue trafficking cases in the United States through international cooperation and engagement in foreign countries. These agencies have trained some 2,000 law enforcement and consular officers, as well as locally employed staff, at embassies and consulates around the world. Closer to home on our border with Mexico, the Departments of Justice and Homeland Security have collaborated with Mexican law enforcement counterparts to exchange leads and evidence, assist victims, and develop high-impact prosecutions under both U.S. and Mexican law.

USAID is one of the largest donors engaged in efforts to counter human trafficking. Since 2001, USAID has programed approximately $180 million in anti-trafficking activities in over 70 countries and regional missions. Throughout all of its work, USAID seeks to address the root causes of exploitation and vulnerability, such as gender and ethnic discrimination, lack of educational and employment opportunities, weak rule of law, and the absence of social welfare safety nets. In Jordan, USAID has integrated countertrafficking activities into a broader human rights program combating sexual- and gender-based violence, early marriage, and child labor among Syrian refugees and host communities affected by the Syrian crisis. With State Department funding, the International Centre for Migration Policy Development is assessing the impact of the Syrian war on trafficking in persons in Syria and the surrounding region (Iraq, Jordan, Lebanon, and Turkey).

In Bangladesh, along with providing training and technical assistance to a range of government officials, USAID has worked to improve community awareness of the risks of human trafficking throughout the country. Local government officials, teachers, parents, students, and community leaders have learned how to prevent human trafficking and support the needs of survivors. USAID also has helped prospective migrant workers protect themselves from deception and abuse through awareness campaigns and trainings on the overseas recruitment process, worker registration, and other risks they may face. USAID continues to train media professionals, NGOs and independent journalists on investigative reporting, story development, and human rights with a focus on migrant worker rights. Complementary TIP Office programming has supported the development and distribution of an anti-trafficking law enforcement training toolkit and hands-on training for 45 Bangladeshi law enforcement officials on the toolkit's practical application. In

Dhaka, Bogra, and Jessore, 258 trafficking survivors so far have received State Department supported shelter, rehabilitation, and reintegration services.

In 2013, Congress gave the State Department a new innovative tool to combat trafficking of children, the Child Protection Compacts (CPC). The compacts can help build sustainable and effective systems of justice, prevention, and protection. I am pleased to tell you that the TIP Office is moving forward to propose the first Child Protection Compact Partnership—to be developed and implemented jointly with the Government of Ghana. This Compact Partnership will include developing a collaborative plan to implement new and more effective policies and programs to reduce child trafficking and improve child protection in Ghana. Several strong civil society organizations are currently working to address child sex trafficking and forced labor in Ghana and, in addition to the Ghanaian Government, the TIP Office expects to engage multiple partners to fulfill the promise of this first Partnership.

Our international partners—including civil society, other governments, and international organizations—play an essential role in making each step forward possible. In the Asia-Pacific region, Australia has taken on a leadership role with its Australia-Asia Program to Combat Trafficking in Persons, a 5-year AUD50 million program to support the Association of Southeast Asian Nations (ASEAN) and seven Southeast Asian countries in developing and implementing criminal justice responses to trafficking in persons. In addition, Australian police regularly conduct trainings to combat child sex tourism and other forms of human trafficking across the Asia-Pacific region. ASEAN under the Government of Burma's chairmanship chose to highlight antitrafficking priorities in 2014.

The European Union is strengthening antitrafficking efforts across its member states through the issuance and enforcement of its 2011 antitrafficking directive, as well as the 2012 directive establishing minimum standards of support to victims of crime. Sweden has allocated millions of dollars in antitrafficking funds in recent years, including in grants to international organizations such as UNICEF and the International Organization for Migration. The Government of the United Kingdom has committed to increase antitrafficking engagement in select countries around the world and will build on current antitrafficking programming including ''Work in Freedom''—a 5-year, approximately $15 million initiative implemented by the ILO to prevent trafficking for labor exploitation of 100,000 women and girls in South Asia by targeting known routes used for the trafficking of migrant workers from South Asia to the Gulf States.

In December, with U.S. support, the Organization for Security and Co-operation in Europe (OSCE) launched its ''Handbook on Preventing Domestic Servitude in Diplomatic Households,'' which is relevant for all international organizations and reaches beyond the OSCE region. Also in December of last year, member states of the Organization of American States revised the organization's ''Work Plan to Combat Trafficking in Persons in the Western Hemisphere'' for the 2015–2018 timeframe. The revised, robust plan includes awareness training for diplomatic personnel, protections against trafficking in government procurement of goods and services, greater oversight of recruitment and placement agencies, and inclusion of trafficking survivors' input in the development of victim assistance policies and programs.

Civilian security and human rights are closely interwoven, and promoting security is often a key means of supporting human rights. Crises increase vulnerabilities to trafficking, as people are displaced, lose income sources and community support systems, and seek physical and economic security for themselves and their families. The breakdown of social and government structures leaves populations defenseless as protections are reduced and options for recourse disappear. In the fight against human trafficking, the State Department looks at the challenge from a holistic foreign policy perspective. We are increasingly mainstreaming antitrafficking elements into other foreign assistance programs. Our antitrafficking programs rely on broader U.S. supported reforms in rule of law, community security, and conflict prevention. The reality is that conflicts and ineffective states give rise to trafficking and allow it

to persist. We must address these underlying causes to win this fight. This is a critical component of the State Department and USAID's work. The U.S. Government works diligently to prevent and stabilize conflicts, and, where it cannot, to help refugees and the internally displaced. These activities complement our strategic efforts in fighting human trafficking. Where the United States, foreign partners, and civil society can help address state weakness, we provide a more stable and effective platform for protecting citizens. Poor enforcement of labor laws, discrimination, corruption, and restrictions on freedom of association and on other human and labor rights leave people at risk of exploitation, including trafficking. The struggle against modern slavery is one of interconnected threats and opportunities. I am proud of the leading role the United States has played, with strong leadership from Congress, in elevating the global profile of this issue, helping free individuals from modern slavery, and galvanizing the work of others to join in to this critical effort. The road is long in our battle against human trafficking, but working with our global partners, the United States will not relent in our multipronged approach to combat this scourge. We welcome Congress' interest and partnership in overcoming this global challenge.

The CHAIRMAN. Thank you for that great testimony.

And the bulk of the State Department's activities, programmatic and funding, actually falls under your purview, and I know there are a number of different entities that are dealing with this. Could you share with us how they are working with each other, and is there anything that might be done to enhance their ability to do so?

Dr. SEWALL. Thank you for that question, Mr. Chairman.

When I came in as the Under Secretary, one of my goals was to create greater synergy and effectiveness and focus across the different bureaus and offices within my Under Secretariat. And we have been working diligently over the year in which I have had the privilege of serving the U.S. Government to achieve just that. We have a number of priorities that we have identified for the J Under Secretariat, but we are working across the board to ensure closer conversation among all entities, programming coordination at the outset, and layered approaches to problems. So let me give you a couple of examples of the ways in which different elements within the State Department are, even though they do not have ''trafficking'' in their title, working in support of the TIP Office and its goals.

INL provides some $4 million to help train law enforcement personnel, prosecutors, and judges to investigate and prosecute trafficking crimes. And this training includes both direct training on trafficking in persons, but it is also incorporated into training on rule of law, anticorruption, law enforcement, border security, or criminal justice. Sometimes this is provided by DHS or international organizations such as UNODC or IOM.

The antitrafficking training is also included in the international law enforcement academies. They are known as ILEA's, and they are scattered around the world. And so that is another institutional way to spread both awareness and skills to combat the trafficking problem.

The Bureau of Democracy, Human Rights, and Labor also promotes internationally recognized labor standards. It targets forced labor directly. It also engages stakeholders to address some of the underlying conditions that can give rise to, or exacerbate, trafficking. So in 2013, DRL supported almost $3 million of activities in Jordan, Pakistan, Sri Lanka, Haiti, and East Asia-Pacific, and they were working with the TIP Office in that work.

They are planning to fund a program that partners with private companies to encourage increased supply chain transparency, monitoring, and accountability, and they will be focusing on working conditions in that.

And then the Bureau of Population, Refugees, and Migration is working closely to integrate prevention and response to human trafficking into humanitarian assistance. This has become a new way of thinking about early intervention to quickly register people, to quickly identify those who are at risk and those who are potential victims and provide services early on. And that has been worked through IOM as well as through the Return, Reintegration, and Family Reunification Program for victims of trafficking, which helped 327 eligible family members join trafficking victims with T visa status in the United States and helped five survivors voluntarily return home.

So these are some of the ways that a broader conversation across different bureaus and offices combine to work on different and mutually supporting elements of the problem.

The CHAIRMAN. I know that entities like Daesh, or ISIL, enslave people, and I realize this is a minor part of the 27 million we know are affected by this. But could you tell us: do these types of entities help further their efforts through human trafficking? Are they taking advantage of this same kind of thing? I do not want to spend a lot of time on it. Because of its currency though, I thought I would just ask.

Dr. SEWALL. Sure. I think if your question, is are terrorist organizations able to exploit ungoverned space in conflict in order to commit crimes of trafficking, the answer is absolutely, ''Yes.''

The CHAIRMAN. Now, are they doing that to fund their activities?

Dr. SEWALL. We do not have particularly good data on that, Mr. Chairman. I think to the extent that we know that profit is made, it certainly represents profit. We do not know the extent of that profit. We do not know exactly how it is used. But clearly there is monetary gain being made when women and children are being advertised as for sale and their price lists are made available through the Internet.

The CHAIRMAN. One of the things we have seen in the field is that rule of law is one of the best ways, if not the best way, to combat this where you hold perpetrators accountable. Do you agree that that is one of the best ways to deal with this issue and to curtail the activity?

Dr. SEWALL. I do, Senator. The reality is that trafficking in persons is a crime, and therefore, the most sustainable and effective way to combat it is to encourage governments to develop the appropriate laws and the appropriate methods of ensuring justice in order to both prosecute and punish those who perpetrate the crime but also deter it in the future. And so rule of law is absolutely vital. So much of what the Department does is, in fact, in support of a rule of law, and I see that as very integral to the antitrafficking cause.

The CHAIRMAN. Last week, when we had a hearing, Senator Menendez and I happened to be meeting with a public official from a country where we knew this was an issue. And so Senator Menendez actually brought it up in that meeting. I guess one of my questions is—obviously there are ways of leveraging this. I mean, just awareness. I know as we meet with people where we know in their own countries this is happening a great deal, it makes a difference.

How are we leveraging through our diplomatic efforts around the world awareness and actually implementation of policies to really cause this to be lessened?

Dr. SEWALL. That is a great question, and it is really central to the work of the State Department. I mean, the Trafficking in

Persons Report is a tool, and it has been, I think, an enormously successful tool. I am extremely gratified by the impact that it has had. But it is also a roadmap for the day-to-day diplomacy that the Department conducts.

I think that it is fair to say that the Secretary's view is that we have an obligation to be raising trafficking issues as part of our daily discourse and that the beauty of having the Trafficking in Persons Office within the State Department and so focused on leveraging the tools of foreign policy and daily diplomacy is that we can keep it on the radar screen in a way that is much more consistent and tied to a broader American agenda than the TIP Report on its own would be able to do.

The CHAIRMAN. And I know right now—this is my last point I guess—this Trafficking in Persons Office really does not have anybody who is the Ambassador at Large, if you will. I assume that you have taken on those responsibilities and we can count on you, in spite of not having someone there, to continue pursuing it heavily.

Dr. SEWALL. We are looking to fill that position as quickly as we can. But I will tell you that last year during the TIP Report final process, I was deeply engaged even with an ambassador there, and I look forward to staying deeply engaged in the time ahead even after we have an Ambassador at Large.

The CHAIRMAN. Thank you. Thanks for your commitment and testimony today.

Senator Menendez.

Senator MENENDEZ. Thank you, Mr. Chairman.

In November 2014, the Government Accountability Office published a report on efforts to combat trafficking on U.S. Government contracts overseas entitled ''Human Trafficking: Oversight of Contractors' Use of Foreign Workers in High-Risk Environments Needs to be Strengthened.''

The GAO investigators spoke to migrant workers on U.S. contracts overseas who had paid an equivalent of up to 1 year's wages to unsavory recruiters in order to secure their jobs.

So as we are talking about trafficking and modern day human slavery, it is pretty mind-boggling that on U.S. Government contracts we might have an iteration of that.

So how does State ensure that U.S. Government contracts overseas are not used as a vehicle for trafficking workers?

Dr. SEWALL. Thanks for that question, Senator.

We are leading, for example, and we have begun in the context of the Executive order that I mentioned in my testimony working first and foremost on our internal supply chain. So as of the Executive order and similar provisions in law, Federal contractors and subcontractors, as well as their employees, are prohibited from deceiving employers about key terms and conditions of employment. They are prohibited from charging employees recruitment fees, and they are prohibited from denying employees access to their identity documents, as well as a host of other things.

Senator MENENDEZ. What is the date of that Executive order?

Dr. SEWALL. I am sorry?

Senator MENENDEZ. What was——

Dr. SEWALL. To be honest, I am not sure how to pronounce, whether it is 13, 627 or whether it is 1, 3, 6, 2, 7, but those are the numbers of it. It is the Federal acquisition regulation rule that implements Executive Order 13627.

So this is something that has been implemented in order to address precisely these kinds of problems. Federal contractors now will need to certify that they have their compliance plans in place, and they will be conducting in-depth mapping of their supply chains, expanding control over recruitment schemes, making available safe and independent grievance mechanisms. And we will continue to be engaging on this issue, including in the context of our ongoing work to develop a national action plan on responsible business——

Senator MENENDEZ. All right. Well, I am informed that the Executive order was issued before the GAO's report.

But as in anything, we can have all the laws in the world and all the Executive orders in the world. It is enforcement that matters in order to send a very clear message that we would, as a government, not tolerate in our own supply chain having that. So I hope we are going to pay particular attention to that.

How does the Department of State work with its partners to strengthen source country policies, for example, places like Bangladesh and Nepal, to prevent fraudulent recruitment practices? Because in the previous hearing that we had, it was a big element of these recruiters or a big part of the challenge we have here. So do we have any specific focus on that?

Dr. SEWALL. We do. Yes, we do, and it is both an issue of bilateral concern but it is also an issue that we support in a more integrated way but we are not directly running that process. So let me walk you through that.

We engage with both sending countries and with destination countries to underscore their responsibilities under the Palermo Protocol and to combat trafficking. And so that is a dialogue, the content of which is contingent on which country and what the circumstances are.

But in addition, we have been encouraging those countries to have a dialogue between both sending and destination countries about how the issues interact with one another. So, for example, the Colombo Process is a nascent dialogue that has been developed between the gulf countries and the South and Southeast Asian nations. A subset of that is the Abu Dhabi Dialogue in which we are just beginning to facilitate that kind of exchange.

And this is an ongoing area. I think it is an area, frankly, Senator, that we are going to be spending more time on and more attention to because we are looking at some big-focusing international events coming up that will provide a very useful forum to raise some issues that are very important to raise. And so it is an area in which I am looking forward to engaging with others in the State Department to focus more on.

Senator MENENDEZ. Okay.

Now, the Trafficking in Persons Report, we have all recognized, is a significant tool in our efforts here. And the chairman referred to the fact that we have no Ambassador at Large in that role. So I assume that your answer to him is that you are personally going to protect the integrity of the TIP Report overall and especially with regard to particular countries that may be subject to intense political pressure within the building?

Dr. SEWALL. Yes. I was involved in the process last year. I am very proud of the process that transpired last year. I look forward to participating in a process that has similar integrity this year.

Senator MENENDEZ. Are there particular countries whose trends you find concerning?

Dr. SEWALL. I think it best to say that we are compiling data on the countries, and that it is very hard for us to identify trends until we get the full amount. As you will be aware, at the end of a reporting period, we tend to get a whole lot more data than we necessarily got along the way. So I think it might be premature to talk about trends. But I think in general we have seen trends going in both directions, and that is one of the biggest advantages of having the annual report process is that we are able to then reflect that in the findings.

Senator MENENDEZ. I hope when you do the report that you would share with the committee insights as to trends that you see developing, whatever those trends may be. It would be very helpful.

Dr. SEWALL. Absolutely.

Senator MENENDEZ. Finally, according to the State Department's own Trafficking in Persons Report, the Government of Cuba does not fully comply with the minimum standards for the elimination of trafficking and is not making significant efforts to do so. It continues to be a source country for adults and children subjected to sex trafficking and conscripts doctors and medical personnel to work overseas under conditions that resemble forced labor. As a matter of fact, that happens to be the number one source of income to the Castro regime is forcing doctors to go abroad and work and then having the payment for those doctors sent back to Cuba.

So between that—and Voyeur magazine had an article, Sex Trafficking Capital of the World,'' several years back about Cuba. Can you tell me whether or not trafficking has been raised and prioritized throughout the administration's new engagement with Havana?

Dr. SEWALL. Yes, absolutely.

Senator MENENDEZ. And how so?

Dr. SEWALL. So, first of all, we have been in an ongoing dialogue with Cuban Government officials. We have met on multiple occasions over the past year to share information on efforts to combat human trafficking. And we expect that that engagement will continue and deepen over time because we do share a commitment to addressing it.

But as you said, government complicity in trafficking is one of the most nefarious and troubling aspects of trafficking in persons. And so that does not mean that this will be an easy conversation, but it will be, as all dialogues are, frank and open. We would like to take advantage of any opening that we have to prompt the Cuban authorities to make progress on trafficking, but the problems, as you pointed out, are severe.

Senator MENENDEZ. I would note, Mr. Chairman, that the Secretary's response suggests that the government is complicit in trafficking, and that makes it all the more—in my mind, one thing is to have a blind eye to what is happening in your country. The other thing is to be complicit in the trafficking. And that is the reality of Cuba.

Thank you for your answer.

The CHAIRMAN. Thank you, sir.

Senator Gardner.

Senator GARDNER. Thank you, Mr. Chairman. Thank you for the hearing again.

Thank you, Madam Under Secretary, for being here today.

I believe the United States should set an example on eradicating the scourge of modern day slavery and human trafficking worldwide, that we need to set that example. We have to be the example here at home so we can show our partners abroad that we have done the work ourselves that we need to.

That is why I am concerned that right here in the United States, the National Human Trafficking Resource Center hotline received nearly four times as many calls in 2013, as recently as 2013, as they did in 2008, with calls rising from 5,748 to 20,000, almost 21,000 calls in 2013 alone.

During the last week's panel, the witness from Humanity United stated in his written testimony that estimates suggest that as many as 300,000 U.S. children are at risk of being trafficked into the commercial sex trade.

I mentioned last week as well work that we have done in Colorado with the Colorado Organization for Victims Assistance. They are 100 percent funded right now, I believe, through the Office of Victims of Crime. They have done a lot of work with a number of victims of modern day slavery and continue to work as well as a subcontractee for the United States Committee on Refugees and Immigrants. And I think there is an issue that they are trying to work out right now through this committee as an OVC grantee and whether or not they can utilize the refugee and immigrant funding for OVC victims in the grantee office. So perhaps we could talk a little bit about some of those issues as well as we work through that and get your help with Justice on this.

They have done a lot of work in terms of setting and meeting the metrics required to help assure funding is going toward victims of trafficking. Would you agree, though, that we need to do more here in the United States to increase our efforts to combat human trafficking so they would be a better example abroad?

Dr. SEWALL. Well, I will begin by expressing humility in the sense that domestic trafficking is not my focus as a State Department official.

Senator GARDNER. I understand.

Dr. SEWALL. And as with any truly egregious human rights violation, there is almost always more that can be done.

I think one of the difficulties that we have again in dealing with many of the problems where victims are often hidden or there is sometimes a real sense of shame that is associated with being a victim, where there are multiple layers that can keep people entrapped in slavery, it is sometimes very difficult both to understand the extent of the problem and then to understand when we learn more, whether that means there is an increase or whether that means that more people have become emboldened to tell their story and seek help.

So I appreciate your concern and I am confident that whatever we can do to help victims, of which there are many, will be welcomed. I cannot speak to anything more specific than that about the domestic——

Senator GARDNER. I understand. No, thank you. I understand.

And are you familiar with the Tier 3 list of countries in the reports that talk about their responses to trafficking?

Dr. SEWALL. Generally speaking. I would probably have to refresh myself, but I can flip to appropriate tab.

Senator GARDNER. Sure. No problem.

You know, these are the most persistent violators of U.S. antihuman trafficking laws and subject to U.S. sanctions under the Trafficking Victims Protection Act, including the withdrawal of nonhumanitarian, non-trade-related foreign assistance.

There is a letter here from the White House dated September 18, 2014. It mentions several nations whether it is Cuba, Russia, others in terms of Tier 3 sanctions.

Could you talk about the economic impact that these sanctions have had on the targeted countries and how much U.S. assistance to these states has been blocked?

Dr. SEWALL. Sure, I can. Do you want me to run through——

Senator GARDNER. Maybe perhaps a few highlights. I mean, for instance, Cuba is listed here. Saudi Arabia is listed here. Just perhaps in Tier 3.

Dr. SEWALL. So the restrictions on educational and cultural exchanges for Cuba were waved. In many cases, the full restrictions apply, but in many cases these countries have also been sanctioned for other reasons. So there is no additional tangible impact, but nonetheless, they have not been waved. So it is country by country.

Senator GARDNER. If they have already been sanctioned for other causes and we are sanctioning them again under this, are they effective? Are they accomplishing what we are trying to do, or are there other things that we need to be doing?

Dr. SEWALL. Well, you know, to be honest, I am not sure that it is the sanctions per se that have the impact, although again it is very specific country by country. I think that the real impact of the TIP Report lies with countries that recognize that they are failing their citizens and see the designation and the criticism as an impetus to make change. We have many ways of engaging. The TIP Report is one tool. Sanctions are another tool. Sanctions are going to matter to some countries more than others, and they are going to matter for different reasons.

I think personally that it is the way the United States has been able to play a leading role in elevating this international norm and then hold countries that purport to be committed to international norms to realize them. As the Senator was saying, the difference between having a law and enforcing a law or the difference between saying that you have signed the protocol and then implementing the law—I think those in many ways are the most tangible results that we have.

So I have been, to be perfectly honest, astonished by the impact that many elements of the whole TVPA have had, and they play different roles in different contexts.

Senator GARDNER. Thank you, Mr. Chairman.

The CHAIRMAN. Senator Shaheen.

Senator SHAHEEN. Thank you, Mr. Chairman.

Under Secretary Sewall, it is nice to see you back in the Government.

Dr. SEWALL. Great to see you, Senator.

Senator SHAHEEN. Yes. We had an opportunity to work together at the Kennedy School, and I saw the great work that you did there.

It was really hearing from students at the Kennedy School that I think first opened my eyes to the issue of trafficking in persons. I had not really been aware and it had not crystallized as something that was occurring in the prevalence that it does around the world until I listened to some of those young people talking about it.

And so what more can we do? You have talked about the programs that the State Department is doing to address trafficking, but what more can we do to make people aware of the extent to which this is an issue and the need for all of us to be aware of it and to call attention if we see anything that we think contributes to trafficking?

Dr. SEWALL. Thanks for that question.

I think for many people the access point for the emotional and intellectual connection to trafficking really is an individual story. And I think one of the things that has been interesting to me, just as I move around in the subway in Washington and I see the Blue Campaign pictures, and you can imagine the story of this person, I think those are very effective ways that we have found to raise general awareness.

Some of the work that the State Department has funded to catalyze social media tools like the Slavery Footprint example that I mentioned are also extremely useful.

I think it is very valuable, as we put a human face on the trafficking problem, that we then tie that to other problems that are more abstract. So we can talk about failed states and ungoverned space, but what does it allow? This is what it allows. Like you, when I met with Yazidis—their community was subjected to horrible human rights abuse, including trafficking in sexual slavery— their story ties that particular crime to a broader conflict and tries to connect the two. So in what is sometimes seen as a very abstract, ''over there'' foreign policy, to be honest, I see a way for trafficking to connect people to the importance of U.S. engagement internationally because it is through the voice of our Government and our posts and our ambassadors that we are able to represent American outrage about this crime.

So I think we do it bit by bit. We do it at a lot of different layers. There is always room to do more, but I really do appreciate your commenting on the power of the story. I think that is part of what has allowed this crime to become so much of a focus because survivors tell stories and the stories are extraordinarily compelling.

And we at the State Department will continue to try to tell and amplify their stories.

Senator SHAHEEN. Thank you.

As we are talking about the products that we use in the developed world that often are available because of trafficked persons, are we addressing that issue as we are looking at the two major trade agreements that we are negotiating now, TTIP and the TTP, and can you talk about how we have addressed it in those agreements?

Dr. SEWALL. I can talk in some detail, but some of these negotiations are still ongoing.

Senator SHAHEEN. Right. I appreciate that.

Dr. SEWALL. So obviously I cannot predict the future.

So for all of these—we talked about the way in which the trafficking issue relies to some extent on a substructure of rule of law. And part of the advantage that we have, as we negotiate these trade agreements, is that they are designed to clarify and hold to account in the formal agreement basic international labor standards. And so to the extent that we are trying to focus on trafficking as a particular element of violation of that regime, getting that regime in place is hugely powerful. And I think that is in no small part what underlies the administration's commitment to trying to put on paper in formal agreements both of these processes. And then they in turn, as we negotiate them, become another forum and another carrot, if you will, to raise the specific of trafficking in another platform for pushing it. So I see it as very much consistent with the broader goals of the antitrafficking community.

Senator SHAHEEN. That is great. And how are we working with our European allies to address this issue and to what extent is it more or less prevalent in Europe than in the United States or North America?

[The written response submitted by Dr. Sewall follows:]

We work closely with our European partners to combat trafficking in persons, both in the region and globally. The State Department regularly engages European governments to share best practices in combating trafficking, as well as assist each other through trainings, technical assistance, and law enforcement working groups. We also collaborate with our European partners in multilateral fora, such as the U.N., OSCE, and Council of Europe, in order to build stronger global norms on countering human trafficking.

Unfortunately, it is exceedingly difficult to produce reliable data on the prevalence of human trafficking. The sampling methodologies common among researchers today are not well-suited for studying trafficking, as the victims are largely hidden. The State Department noted in the 2014 TIP Report that governments and civil society organizations reported identifying over 44,000 victims of human trafficking in 2013; however, the International Labor Organization estimated that there are 20.9 million victims globally. The hidden nature of many human trafficking crimes impairs researchers' ability to estimate prevalence of human trafficking.

Dr. SEWALL. I cannot speak to prevalence because it is so hard to generalize country by country, transit versus source. It is hard to generalize. I can get you more information on that, and I would be happy to do so.

I think it is fair to say that this has become—in the same way that our engagement with countries that experience enormous problems as a source country or as a destination country, this has become also a generic topic of collaboration with likeminded countries that are similarly concerned. And so Australia, the U.K.

come to mind as examples where the governments are very much seized with these issues, very engaged diplomatically on these issues, raising them in the EU context, working on them in the context of specific programs that they run.

It is again part of what the American people can, I think, be very proud of by raising this item on the international normative agenda. Others have come to work on it in a much more applied and commonly articulated way. And so I think these really are multiplier effects that we are able to have working together with partners.

Senator SHAHEEN. Well, thank you very much for the great work that you and the Department are doing.

Dr. SEWALL. It is a team, and many of them are behind me, but on their behalf, you are welcome.

Senator SHAHEEN. Thank you all.

And thank you, Mr. Chairman and Senator Menendez, for organizing this hearing.

The CHAIRMAN. Thank you.

Senator Cardin.

Senator CARDIN. Thank you, Mr. Chairman.

The title of this hearing, I think, really speaks to our mission, "Ending Modern Slavery," the critical priority that this must be for our country, and the importance of U.S. leadership, because we know we are not going to make progress internationally if the United States does not maintain a very strong position.

So I want to drill down a little bit on what Senator Shaheen said. I very much respect the work that you do and that your team does. It is critically important. You have been a voice for people around the world, and you have brought about significant improvements around the world. And we very much appreciate that.

But as Senator Menendez said, there are certain opportunities that you have that you have really got to take advantage of. Senator Menendez mentioned Cuba. There is an opportunity there. We have their attention. And I must tell you, as things become more normal and trade starts, you lose that leverage.

So I appreciate your answer to Senator Shaheen, and I agree with you that in the trade agreements we hope we will see stronger labor protections, greater emphasis on good governance and anticorruption efforts, and enforcement of these provisions. But it would give me a little bit more comfort if I knew your views on why Malaysia is a Tier 3 country and still a candidate for TPP. What changes can we expect to see implemented in Malaysia before the trade agreement is signed, or is there sufficient enforcement in the trade agreement being negotiated so that Malaysia will not be a Tier 3 country enjoying a trade agreement with the United States. What assurances can you give us?

Dr. SEWALL. What I can do—Senator Cardin, as you will appreciate, I am not running the trade negotiations. So what I can do as a servant of the United States Government but one part of a team is take your question back and answer it more fully in consultation with my colleagues that are running the trade negotiations. But I would be delighted to do that, sir.

[The written response submitted by Dr. Sewall follows:]

In the Trans-Pacific Partnership (TPP) talks, we are seeking strong, enforceable commitments on fundamental labor rights. This includes commitments on the elimination of all forms of forced or compulsory labor and on the worst forms of child labor, including forced child labor and the commercial sexual exploitation of children. Officials from USTR and the Departments of State and Labor have engaged closely with Malaysia to discuss needed reforms, including related to forced labor. TPP provides the U.S. Government with an additional platform to raise these issues and seek necessary reforms.

Senator CARDIN. I thank you for that.

I just remind you that there are rumors going around here that we may be asked to vote on trade promotion authority within the next couple weeks. So there is not a lot of time to get back to us on this. Normally, we would put in trade promotion authority what we expect to be accomplished by the trade agreements. And I could be pretty specific as it relates to trafficking, and perhaps you will help me draft language to deal with compliance with the criteria that we use in the TIP Report that we could add to TPA. That might be helpful if the administration is so inclined. But I would like to have specific information on this.

Dr. SEWALL. We will get that to you.

[The written response submitted by Dr. Sewall follows:]

Trade agreements like TPP provide an additional platform to urge other governments to address concerns related to trafficking and forced labor. The administration is committed to continuing to use this platform in this regard.

Senator CARDIN. Thank you.

I would also like to have recommendations from you as to how we can improve the Trafficking in Persons Report. You mentioned that as you get closer to the publication dates, you see activities. It would also I think be helpful if we could figure out how we could perhaps improve the reporting requirements in an effort to make this tool an internationally recognized tool. How can we strengthen it?

Dr. SEWALL. I would be happy to talk about that.

I think the first thing that I will tell you—and again, I am reflecting the work of the team—is that from our perspective, we are always seeking to strengthen the report.

One of the difficulties—and I will say this just from my past life as an academic—is that when you have a law that has very specific requirements and you have a very careful system for reaching conclusions, you have to write in a way that sometimes makes it hard for the reader to do what Senator Shaheen was talking about, which is really connect viscerally to the problem. In other words, there is a lot of formula in the report. And so trying to harmonize the need to be very specific and responsive to the law and its requirements and creating something that is more able to connect to people on a human level I think is a constant challenge within that report.

I also think that there is a danger always in compiling these reports that you have basically the same list of failings for countries that are truly challenged and they may all share the same list of challenges, but three pieces may be particularly important in this country and three very different issues may be the center of the problem in another country. And I think we are struggling to try to find a way to reflect that without not fully capturing all of the data that we have. That is another tension in the report.

There are some issues like child marriage that we think about the human rights reporting and we think about the trafficking in persons reporting, and we wonder how best to reflect those issues.

So those are ways in which we grapple with trying to make both a more useful and user friendly report, and the team is constantly asking itself how it can improve the product.

Senator CARDIN. Do you know whether there has been a sharing of the standards that you use in evaluating countries under the TIP Report with our trade negotiators so that they have more objective ways of determining progress made in good governance in countries dealing with trafficking?

Dr. SEWALL. That is a very good question. I do not know the answer, but I will undertake to make sure that we do just that.

Senator CARDIN. If you could get back to me on that, I would appreciate it.

Dr. SEWALL. Sure.

[The written response submitted by Dr. Sewall follows:]

The Department of State has consulted closely with USTR throughout the TPP negotiations. The Department has reviewed the TIP Report with USTR and coordinated with them on how to ensure that the TPP agreement includes strong provisions on eliminating forced labor and discouraging trade in goods made with forced labor.

Senator CARDIN. My last question deals with transparency. Some of my colleagues have already talked about that. We have found that transparency works well. When we look at multinational companies that have access to our markets, the chain of supply and the companies that they have dealt with and their labor practices, et cetera, the more transparency that you can show on those issues, the less chance we will see support for trafficking in labor. Is that an area in which you are also talking with the trade negotiators to make sure that we have more transparency in the countries that we are dealing with, that we do not see our multinational companies supporting trafficking?

Dr. SEWALL. You know, we have been able to use—I am sure you are aware of this—transparency in a number of different contexts, you know, the extractive industries, for example, in terms of creating greater awareness of inputs and outputs. Transparency, as a general principle of governance, is something that the United States has been extremely active on. The Open Government Partnership is committed to basically pushing the bar up, helping countries become more transparent in all elements of governance. So I think it is fair to say that the U.S. view in general is very much in accord with your own, Senator, which is that more transparency is helpful.

Again, I have not had a specific conversation with the trade negotiators about that, but I can add that to the now fulsome roster of issues to raise with them. [Laughter.]

[The written response submitted by Dr. Sewall follows:]

Ensuring transparency in supply chains in order to discourage trade in goods produced by forced labor is a priority for the Department. Under TPP, we are working to include new commitments for our trading partners to discourage trade in goods produced by forced labor. More broadly, the Department has been actively engaged in efforts to promote responsible business conduct, which includes transparency and respect for human rights, in global supply chains, including through the National Action Plan on Responsible Business Conduct announced by President Obama last

September. We regularly coordinate with USTR and other relevant U.S. agencies on these issues.

Senator CARDIN. I appreciate that very much, and I look forward to working with you and you getting back to me. Thanks.

Dr. SEWALL. Thank you.

The CHAIRMAN. Thank you, Senator.

I know Senator Menendez had a closing question and comment.

Senator MENENDEZ. Thank you, Mr. Chairman.

I want to follow up on Senator Cardin's point because this issue boggles my mind sometimes. And I know from your confirmation hearing, which I was privileged to chair, you are eminently qualified for the position you now hold. But sometimes in an institution like the State Department, you have to have sharper elbows. And to hear the answer about Malaysia, as by way of one example, as we are negotiating, I mean, a trade agreement should not have already raised these trafficking issues to countries that are on the TIP Report list. Because the fact of the matter is that it undermines, I think, our moral authority to say that we are willing to do business with you but, you know, on this question—you know, you are on our Trafficking In Persons list, but we are willing to do business with you. That is a tough proposition.

So I would hope that you would take a more activist role in looking at how you take your TIP Report, which I think we all agree is a very powerful tool, and look at other elements of our Government to make sure that we are in harmony with what we are trying to pursue. Otherwise, whether it be contracting, whether it be negotiations for trade or other elements, I think we erode the very essence of what we are trying to pursue. And so in some respects, I do not want us to be duplicitous in the way in which we look at this because otherwise I am not sure that we are going to achieve a goal that I know the chairman is very singularly focused on here and which I share his views on.

Dr. SEWALL. Senator Menendez, I think it is an excellent point. I do want to clarify that we do distribute the TIP Report. It is very much part of the woof and warp of the State Department. Typically—and I do not mean this to be a pedantic, bureaucratic answer, but I do not want to leave you with the impression that people are unaware of the report or that the issues—for example, the case of Malaysia, people have not discussed it in the context of trade. I was asked a question about whether I had.

So the bureaucratic way this would work is that the regional bureaus, which work on all elements of a given country's issue, are very much aware of the TIP Report because they are very deeply engaged in the adjudication process every year. They are very aware and they are working with the trade bureaus. So I think it is an absolutely important point.

And I take Senator Cardin's exhortation for us to go and add an additional conversation from a functional lens, but those conversations do happen. They just happen separately, and I did not want to be speaking for the Department as a whole rather than my own role.

Senator MENENDEZ. And I understand what you are saying, but let me maybe try to crystallize my point. That a regional bureau raises the question or knowledge that the TIP Report says this about this country who you are negotiating with is one thing. That the Under Secretary for this position raises that at a level that is more among equals is a much more powerful set of circumstances.

Dr. SEWALL. Point taken.

The CHAIRMAN. Well, listen, I want to thank you for your efforts. I think you have been an excellent witness. I appreciate what you are doing at the State Department. Obviously, we want to see things move along even more quickly, and I think we are going to be working toward an end here very soon that will be very complementary to what you are doing. And we thank you again for your service to our country, for being here today, for being an outstanding witness, and we look forward to working with you on a continual basis.

Dr. SEWALL. Thank you, Mr. Chairman. It was a pleasure to join you all.

The CHAIRMAN. Thank you.

The hearing is adjourned.

[Whereupon, at 3:11 p.m., the hearing was adjourned.]

ADDITIONAL MATERIAL SUBMITTED FOR THE RECORD

RESPONSES OF SARAH SEWALL TO QUESTIONS SUBMITTED BY SENATOR ROBERT MENENDEZ

Questions a-c. In November 2014, the Government Accountability Office published a report on efforts to combat trafficking on U.S. Government contracts overseas— ''Human Trafficking: Oversight of Contractors' Use of Foreign Workers in High-Risk Environments Needs to Be Strengthened.'' GAO investigators spoke to migrant workers on U.S. contracts overseas who had paid an equivalent of 1 year's wages to unsavory recruiters in order to secure their jobs.

◆a. How does the Department of State ensure that U.S. Government contracts overseas are not used as a vehicle for trafficking workers?

Answer. The State Department takes seriously its responsibility to ensure that its contracts overseas are not being used as a vehicle for trafficking workers. Since 2011, the State Department has issued Procurement Information Bulletins (PIBs) to provide guidance to its Contracting Officers (CO) and Contracting Officer Representatives (COR) on how to monitor contracts for compliance with antitrafficking provisions, and it has enhanced its training as well. The State Department and the Department of Homeland Security developed online training for acquisition professionals across the U.S. Government; a 35-minute course is currently available on the Federal Acquisition Institute's Web site. (Federal agencies are working to update this training now that the FAR rule implementing Executive Order 13627, Strengthening Protections Against Trafficking in Persons in Federal Contracts (E.O. 13627), has been released.)

The State Department revised its Contractor Officer Representative (COR) course to include a detailed discussion on COR responsibilities for managing antitrafficking requirements, and updated its COR Handbook in the Foreign Affairs Handbook to reflect these requirements. A webinar on preventing Trafficking in Persons was developed specifically to target posts identified by the GAO as needing additional guidance.

The State Department strengthened contract review and staff review of procurement files at posts during periodic visits to verify that an antitrafficking clause is included. Contracts sent to Washington from posts for approval are reviewed by Washington staff for inclusion of the antitrafficking clause.

The State Department was an early advocate of prohibiting the charging of recruitment fees to employees because of the potential for abuse. This prohibition was incorporated into E.O. 13627. Now that the Federal Acquisition Regulation (FAR) rule has been issued implementing E.O. 13627, the FAR rule and similar provisions in laws make clear that federal contractors and subcontractors (and their employees) are prohibited from deceiving employees about key terms and conditions of employment; charging employees' recruitment fees; and denying employees' access to identity documents. They are also prohibited from using forced labor and from procuring commercial sex acts in the performance of a contract or subcontract. Federal contractors performing work outside of the United States worth over $500,000 need to maintain compliance plans and certify to the best of their knowledge that neither they, nor any of their subcontractors, have engaged in trafficking or trafficking-related activities. The State Department was instrumental in implementing the GAO report's recommendation to define recruitment fees more clearly through the development of a new governmentwide FAR definition. That change will be promulgated through an impending FAR case.

Finally, the U.S. Government is using all available tools to better assist procurement officers, federal contractors, and other interested corporations. For example, this includes a global project the State Department has funded to Verite, an award-winning labor rights NGO, to research the key sectors and commodities at risk for human trafficking, draft an extensive report summarizing its findings, and develop a set of online, public-facing tools. These resources will enable federal contractors and other businesses to adopt ethical sourcing guidelines and compliance plans that align with E.O. 13627, and will be available in 2015.

    ◆b. How is the Department of State working with transit countries, such as in the Middle East and the gulf, to improve conditions for workers and oversight of contractors recruiting and employing workers in these countries?

Answer. It is the responsibility of governments to hold employers accountable for adhering to labor laws and to prevent the trafficking of workers. Visa sponsorship systems, including the kafala system in effect in many countries in the Middle East, can place significant leverage in the hands of employers and recruitment agencies and create the potential for exploitation. Additionally, labor laws in many parts of the region do not fully apply to migrant workers, in particular migrant domestic workers. The Department continues to encourage governments to pursue reforms of such systems and labor laws. Some governments in the region have announced plans to make such reforms. The Department also continues to encourage governments to better enforce existing laws that prohibit employers from withholding workers' passports and restricting workers' movements, including by denying exit visas, as a means of preventing trafficking abuses.

In 2012, sending and receiving countries agreed—through the Abu Dhabi Dialogue, a collaboration between gulf countries and South and Southeast Asian nations involved in the Colombo Process—to a framework which aims to increase intergovernmental partnerships in a number of areas, including through guidelines on labor recruitment, enforcement of labor standards, training or support throughout the migration process. We also work with international organizations on funding and technical assistance efforts to improve labor governance and respect for internationally recognized worker rights as a key part of preventing extreme abuses such as trafficking in persons.

    ◆c. How is the Department of State working with its partners to strengthen source country policies, such as in Bangladesh and Nepal, including the regulation of recruiting agencies?

Answer. In source countries, the Department advocates, as a key priority, that governments sharply reduce and eventually eliminate recruitment fees and criminally prosecute those suspected of fraudulent recruitment—two practices that increase the vulnerability of migrant workers to forced labor. The Department also advocates for governments to take action to ensure that those intending to migrate for work are informed of their rights and protected throughout the migration process. The Department is currently exploring ways to empower sending countries to have more leverage to protect their workers overseas, for example through effective and transparent MOUs.

Programmatically, the Department provides assistance programming toward these objectives. In Bangladesh, the TIP Office is funding the Solidarity Center, which in partnership with local implementing partners has integrated basic antitrafficking training into the curriculum of the Dhaka Technical Training Center for Migrant Workers, disseminating valuable information on the rights and obligation of migrant workers, the telltale signs of trafficking, and mechanisms for recourse if they find themselves in exploitative and abusive situations overseas. Every month an estimated 1,000 migrant workers receive such training, and so far more than 7,000 migrant workers have benefited from the program. The Bureau of Democracy, Human Rights and Labor (DRL) is in the process of awarding a new project in Bangladesh that will promote core labor standards, including freedom of association and occupational safety and health, and raise the standard of living and promote inclusive economic growth for all Bangladeshi citizens. Additionally, DRL funds the ILO for a project that works to protect the rights of migrant workers through organizing, empowerment activities, enhanced cooperation and trade union support in several countries, including Nepal.

In Nepal, USAID is funding a 5-year project that includes creating Safe Migration Networks and training Network members to increase their ability to promote safe migration. The Department has coordinated with other government and private donors to enhance use of foreign assistance funding and reduce duplication—to more effectively work toward ending these practices that contribute to human trafficking from the region.

Question. Several countries that appear on the lowest tier in the Department of State's Trafficking in Persons Report (TIP) due to severe labor rights violations and forced labor, such as Thailand and Malaysia, currently receive trade preferences from the United States or are part of trade negotiations, including the Trans-Pacific Partnership (TPP).

♦ Is the Department of State engaging with USTR to ensure that the concerns raised in the TIP Report for these countries are addressed before they receive trade preferences?

Answer. The Department promotes and reports on internationally recognized worker rights and efforts to combat human trafficking around the world, including in Thailand and Malaysia.

- In Thailand, we meet regularly with key labor, civil society, and private sector interlocutors to discuss labor conditions in the country, including forced labor, and are in regular contact with USTR on these issues. The elimination of forced labor is a core part of the eligibility criteria of our trade preference programs, including the Generalized System of Preferences. In October 2013, the AFL–CIO submitted a petition seeking the suspension or limitation of Thailand's GSP trade benefits based on alleged shortcomings on worker rights in Thailand, including forced labor. Once Congress acts to reauthorize the GSP program, the administration will decide whether to accept this petition for formal review.
- In Malaysia, officials from Departments of State and Labor and USTR have engaged closely with the Malaysian Government on needed reforms to combat trafficking, including reforms related to forced labor. In the Trans-Pacific Partnership (TPP) talks, we are seeking strong, enforceable commitments on fundamental labor rights. This includes commitments on the elimination of all forms of forced or compulsory labor and on the worst forms of child labor, including forced child labor and the commercial sexual exploitation of children. The Department has reviewed the TIP Report with USTR and coordinated with them on how to better ensure that the TPP agreement includes strong provisions on eliminating forced labor and discouraging trade in goods made with forced labor. Malaysia is not a GSP beneficiary.

Question. Trafficking of domestic workers into the United States by foreign diplomats is a significant concern. NGOs report that domestic workers in the U.S. on A–3 and G–5 visas (special visas reserved for the domestic workers of diplomats and international organization employees respectively) have brought more than 29 federal civil cases alleging human trafficking by their diplomatic employers. Nearly 2 years ago, Secretary Kerry announced that the Department of State would begin conducting screening interviews with domestic workers on special visas to identify abuse. These interviews have not yet begun, and it is my understanding that several of our OSCE partners have been conducting similar interviews with domestic workers employed by diplomats stationed in their countries for several years.

♦ What is the delay in conducting these interviews and what is the schedule for them to take place?

Answer. The Department's initiative to implement annual in-person registration of domestic workers is well underway. The development of this program involved a number of factors to include additional resources, budgetary discussions, and the need for the system to be conducive for the majority of non-English speaking domestic workers employed by foreign diplomatic personnel. We will begin in-person registration of domestic workers in the Washington, DC, area, which has the highest number of workers employed by foreign mission personnel, this summer. Once this program is fully operational in Washington the project will be implemented in New York City followed by other cities throughout the United States. This effort, will serve as an important tool to prevent abuse, and to provide domestic workers an avenue in which to raise to the Department matters of concern related to their employment. Prior to the rollout of the registration system, the Office of the Chief of Protocol will be holding a briefing for foreign deputy chiefs of missions regarding this new requirement. The Department will also host a briefing for domestic workers (without their employers present) to discuss with domestic workers their rights and responsibilities, contract requirements, visa matters, and resources available to them in the event they suffer abuse or mistreatment. The Department has engaged with a number of OSCE partners regarding their interview processes. Consistent with evolving best practices, the Department has determined it would be beneficial to institute a policy of in-person registration for domestic workers on an annual basis to better monitor their welfare. Many OSCE partners deal with domestic worker numbers at a much lower scale within their capitals. The United States is unique in that its program will need to address thousands of workers, many outside of Washington, DC.

Question. There have been a number of high profile cases involving Indian diplomats who have perpetrated severe forms of labor exploitation against their domestic workers, including forced labor and human trafficking. Specifically, we have received credible reports that India is attempting to circumvent protections in the TVPA for A–3/G–5 domestic workers by misclassifying these workers as A–2 visa program-eligible, and that the Department of State is allowing this misclassification by issuing the A–2 visas.

♦ What is the Department of State doing to mitigate these risks? And, are the reports about India misclassifying visas accurate?

Answer. The Department works to ensure that the individuals who come to the United States in the personal employ of, and working in the private residences of, mission members as domestic workers enter the United States with an A–3 or G–5 visa. The legal requirements for A–3 visas, which are for domestic workers, are different than the requirements for A–2 visas. A visa applicant may be issued an A–2 visa only if he or she meets all requirements for A–2 visa issuance. Broadly speaking, A–2 is a visa category for foreign government employees performing official activities for a foreign government. All visa applications are adjudicated by consular officers based on their individual merits. We are happy to provide further briefings, although we cannot discuss specific visa cases.

Question. It is also my understanding that the Government of India is preventing family members of individuals trafficked from India to the U.S. from reuniting with these trafficking victims here in the U.S. Many trafficking victims from India have received T-visas. Their immediate family members have received T-derivative visas, allowing them to come to the U.S. to join their family member. However, the Indian Government has physically blocked victims' families from traveling to the U.S. by seizing passports and turning them away from the airport. This conduct punishes trafficking victims, who have already suffered enormously.

♦ What is the Department of State doing to assure that trafficking victims' families are not prevented from traveling from India to the U.S. to reunite with victims?

Answer. The Department notes that persons who have been trafficked to the United States may be granted T-nonimmigrant status since they are already in the United States and therefore do not require a visa. The Department is very concerned about the Government of India's June 2014 policy that effectively prevents survivors of human trafficking in the United States from reunifying with their families and from receiving the needed support and assistance available from the U.S. Government. The Department of State has expressed its concern over this policy with the Government of India at various levels in Washington and through Mission India, and U.S officials continue to press the Indians to repeal this policy.

Question. The 2014 TIP Report noted that, ''the terrorist organization, Boko Haram, had abducted women and girls in the northern region of Nigeria, some of whom it later subjected to domestic servitude, forced labor, and sex slavery through forced marriages to its militants.'' We cannot address the issue of trafficking by Boko Haram without tackling the larger gaps that allowed violent extremism to take root in northern Nigeria.

♦ Please address current policies and programs that the Department of State is implementing to counter violent extremism in Nigeria, understanding the myriad problems, such as trafficking, that arise in its wake.

Answer. As President Obama outlined in his remarks on February 19 during the White House Summit on Countering Violent Extremism, the United States will continue to pursue a comprehensive, multidisciplinary approach to countering violent extremism, in Nigeria and elsewhere. Our approach includes several types of policies and programs.

First, we are continuing to work with the governments of Nigeria and neighboring countries to help them build up their security forces so that they can push back against Boko Haram and prevent the emergence of ungoverned spaces where terrorists find safe haven. We are also helping them meet civilian security and humanitarian needs. These efforts include support for the creation of the National Information Center, which is designed to improve communications between the Government of Nigeria and Nigerian citizens, as well as government transparency. In addition, we are helping to amplify voices of tolerance and peace while confronting the warped ideologies espoused by terrorist groups like Boko Haram, especially their attempt to use Islam to justify their violence.

Cameroon, Chad, Niger, and Nigeria were all among the countries at the recent Countering Violent Extremism Summit. On the margins of the summit, the heads of their delegations held a productive and frank discussion with Deputy Secretary Blinken to share concerns and request assistance in their efforts to confront the violent extremism of Boko Haram. The Department is actively considering their requests and continues to emphasize the need for security forces to respect human rights, as well as the need for a civilian protection-focused approach while countering violent extremism (and Boko Haram specifically).

The United States is spending more than $15 million on a range of programs to help local communities in Nigeria, Niger, Chad, and Cameroon counter violent extremism. These programs include funding for the Hausa-language Arewa 24 satellite platform in Northern Nigeria, centered around a 24 hour satellite channel, and resources for smaller programs that are designed to provide positive alternatives, marketable skills and civic engagement opportunities to vulnerable youth. In addition, some of those programs are designed to support local media platforms in providing accurate and timely information and messages that promote reconciliation and nonviolence in northern Nigeria, as well as the monitoring and documenting of human rights abuses, and an early warning system.

Second, we are working to address the grievances that violent extremists exploit, including economic grievances. Boko Haram itself has often cited governmental corruption and inequity of economic development in northern Nigeria in an attempt to justify the violence it perpetrates. And corruption has proven to be a particularly potent recruiting tool for Boko Haram. As underscored by President Obama's National Security Strategy, the U.S. Government is committed to strengthening partnerships that ''promote the recognition that pervasive corruption is a severe impediment to development and global security.'' This is why we continue to work with the Nigerian Government and civil society organizations to institutionalize greater transparency and accountability.

For example, the State Department continues to support a $2.5 million grass roots-driven anticorruption program in Nigeria. The project, entitled Accountable Governance for Justice and Security, is supporting our efforts to counter corruption and transnational organized crime in West Africa. The overall project goal is to build more transparent and accountable governance institutions in both countries' justice and security sectors by enhancing institutional transparency. Specifically, it is building the capacity of civil society and media to more effectively mobilize and equip citizens to engage key government entities (police, judiciaries, etc.) in efforts to prevent impunity for those who commit acts of corruption and transnational crime. Preventing that kind of impunity for corruption is important to advancing the rule of law, preventing economic exclusion of marginalized groups, and, as a result, countering the appeal of extremist messaging. The project is building a more effective civil society network in West Africa for best practices sharing and peer learning on corruption issues such as stolen asset recovery and the use of new crowdsourcing technologies to fight corruption from the grassroots level.

Third, the United States continues to address the political grievances that proponents of violent extremism exploit in Nigeria and surrounding countries. As President Obama underscored at the recent summit, ''when people are oppressed and human rights are denied—particularly along sectarian or ethnic lines—when dissent is silenced, it feeds violent extremism.'' It creates an environment that is ripe for terrorists such as Boko Haram to exploit. To address long-standing grievances, we support programs in Nigeria that promote the rule of law, fair elections and respect for human rights, including freedoms of religion, association, and speech. This support reflects our belief that lasting stability and real security require vibrant, inclusive, and participatory democracy.

While information gathering remains a serious challenge in these insecure environments, the Department continues to monitor the effects of Boko Haram's presence, including trafficking in persons crimes and the recruitment and use of child soldiers in these communities.

Question. In 2013, the Conflict Stabilization Bureau—which is now under your leadership—began a scoping exercise for stabilization programming in Nigeria. We understand that their initial assessment missions and analysis led them to propose an impressive suite of program ideas to dampen the appeal of violent extremism in the North, but due to security restrictions, were not allowed to proceed with the programs. Consequently, the CSO Bureau developed an important and creative conflict prevention program in the Middle Belt to address the ongoing pastoral/herder conflict. If the USG seeks to make an impact in the world's most difficult places, we need to seek opportunities to have a presence there when feasible.

◆ Can you please comment on how the Department of State is working to balance our efforts to prevent the spread of violent extremism in light of current security restrictions we place on our frontline State Department and USAID staff?

Answer. The initiative I recently launched to prevent violent extremism is meant to address sociopolitical drivers of violent extremism before they metastasize into full-fledged support. As part of this initiative the Department will work to identify factors that lead communities to violent extremism, identify communities that are currently vulnerable to its spread, and suggest ways to take diplomatic and programmatic action before it is too late. By definition these are communities that are not yet under the sway of violent extremist organizations and therefore not yet off limits to the Department's diplomats and staff. We would be happy to brief you and your staff on this work.

Where the Department's access to communities and regions has been restricted due to security concerns, we can still try to prevent further entrenchment of extremism, or its spread, by operating through implementing partners who can work more flexibly than U.S. Government personnel in nonpermissive environments. We also work through international organizations, contracted third-country nationals, and third-party governments to close gaps in prevention, mitigation, or stabilization efforts that emerge due to security restrictions. Such methods work best however, when we diversify our diplomatic and programmatic partnerships with a broader range of local stakeholders when we do still have access. Developing these relations and contacts takes time. We as a government should be careful not to make trade-offs or begin retrenching by limiting programs and travel or by losing our contact with local actors too early. Doing so may hasten the very outcome we are hoping to avoid. We need to start understanding and managing risks earlier, and then use this information to stay deeply engaged longer.

Question. We want to commend the work of the DRL Bureau for its forward-looking and strategic surge of assistance to prevent election-related violence in Nigeria. They did not wait until it was too late to begin program work. As we've learned from previous election-related assistance efforts, upstream prevention is critical.

◆ Can you please comment on the Department of State's election and post-election programming efforts in Nigeria in an effort to consolidate peace in the critical post-election period, and to lay a foundation for a transitional period?

Answer. The United States, in a whole of government effort, has engaged at the highest levels with Nigerian candidates, political party leadership, civil society, business leaders, and other prominent individuals to promote peaceful and credible elections in March 2015. Through frequent outreach to key stakeholders in Nigeria, including government officials and civil society members, the State Department has built and/or maintained relationships that will endure beyond the elections in March and April. The State Department will continue to engage at all levels to advance peaceful democratic goals in Nigeria after the elections. Secretary of State Kerry visited Abuja January 25 and met with both President Jonathan and retired General Buhari, reinforcing the importance of pledging publicly to refrain from violence. Assistant Secretary of State for African Affairs Linda Thomas-Greenfield has traveled frequently to Nigeria and led the U.S. delegation to the Bi-National Commission Working Group on elections in February 2014. She will lead our diplomatic elections observation in Abuja.

Over 200 mission staff members will conduct election observation missions during the general elections currently scheduled for March 28 and April 11. The mission is closely coordinating its observation efforts with embassies from like-minded countries and civil society.

The Department is funding U.S. elections observers through the International Republican Institute (IRI) and the National Democratic Institute (NDI) and supported a joint NDI–IRI preelection assessment mission from January 15–20, 2015. Our statement after that assessment outlined several recommendations on communications, election administration, and violence mitigation and steps that various stakeholders could undertake to address those recommendations.

We also are funding a program to strengthen the capacity of target communities and leaders to prevent and respond to religious, ethnosectarian, and political conflict before, during, and after the 2015 elections. Additionally, we have a rapid response mechanism in place that would enable it to do so, should the situation on the ground necessitate a programmatic response.

The U.S. Government has engaged the Nigerian Government, the Independent National Electoral Commission (INEC), and civil society to emphasize the need for a clear and well-coordinated elections security plan, and to offer assistance. An elections security consultant has been deployed to directly support INEC security operations.

Mindful that inaccurate and sensationalist reporting may contribute to post-electoral violence, as in 2011 when an estimated 800 Nigerians were killed over the course of 3 days, the U.S. Government funds programs to help professionalize the media and strengthen the reporting skills of journalists. Additionally, U.S. Government entities have partnered on a conflict prevention and mitigation initiative to reduce the risk of destabilizing election-related violence in the Niger Delta.

We have been providing assistance to Nigeria to strengthen its electoral systems since 1999, and have been consistently working toward this objective since the last Nigerian General Elections in 2011. U.S. Government assistance has been provided in three basic areas: (1) strengthening of the Independent National Electoral Commission (INEC) to organize and carry out elections; (2) training of civil society organizations (CSOs) to conduct domestic election observation, engage with INEC to ensure proper voter education and information, and that electoral processes are fair and adequate; and (3) supporting major political parties to enhance their inclusiveness and to develop strong issues-based platforms.

Questions a-b. NGOs and aid workers have decried the lack of humanitarian assistance to those who have been displaced and forced to flee as refugees due to the Boko Haram crisis. There are reports of Boko Haram recruitment in chronically vulnerable areas of northern Nigeria, as well as further south.

♦a. What is the humanitarian outlook for victims of the Boko Haram crisis?

Answer. Attacks by Boko Haram have increased in intensity and brutality over the past months, with significant civilian impacts. Last year, State Department analysts estimate Boko Haram killed more than 5,000 people—doubling in 1 year the death toll attributable to Boko Haram since 2009. In addition, Boko Haram-engendered fighting has generated an estimated 1 million internally displaced persons (IDPs) within Nigeria's borders, and forced more than 200,000 Nigerian refugees and other nationals to flee to neighboring Niger, Cameroon, and Chad. In fleeing the violence, some have faced a chain of displacement, running to one town only to leave once more as Boko Haram's reach has grown. These attacks strike at the core of every day life—markets, places of worship, and schools—and cast a shadow of fear over communities. As attacks spill over Nigeria's borders, the stability and security of Cameroon, Chad, and Niger are increasingly under threat.

According to the International Organization for Migration (IOM), more than 90 percent of IDPs live in rural and urban host communities while the remaining 10 percent are in camps or camp-like sites. Displaced populations—both IDPs in Nigeria and refugees in neighboring countries—have primarily relied on the generosity of local communities to sustain them, stressing the household resources of those who themselves may be impoverished and facing food insecurity. The Government of Nigeria's National Emergency Management Agency and the State Emergency Management Agencies are providing aid to those living in IDP camps in Nigeria. The U.N. and other aid agencies are working in dangerous and difficult environments in Nigeria and in border areas of Cameroon, Chad, and Niger to provide life-saving emergency shelter, health, water and sanitation, and protection to IDPs, refugees, and other populations of concern affected by the conflict.

♦b. What are the impediments to the U.S.—in coordination with international NGOs and agencies—in undertaking a more robust response?

Answer. The United States is deeply concerned by the growing number of IDPs and refugees fleeing Boko Haram's horrors, and we have been working since the start of the emergency with our international partners to respond to their needs. However, the humanitarian response faces tremendous challenges and, to date, escalating humanitarian needs in the region have not been met with a commensurate increase in support.

The primary challenge in meeting humanitarian needs is the widespread insecurity due to the presence of Boko Haram, which has now launched attacks beyond Nigeria into neighboring Cameroon, Chad, and Niger, including in areas hosting refugees. This insecurity limits the ability of relief agencies to work safely in conflict-affected areas. In addition, the number of competing large-scale crises across the globe have placed an unprecedented level of demand on international aid agencies and resulted in funding and staffing shortages. Local capacity is also very limited. Although the Government of Nigeria's National Emergency Management Agency and the State Emergency Management Agencies are assisting with IDPs and conflict-affected people in Nigeria, they are only reaching those living in IDP camps, an estimated 10 percent of the nearly 1 million IDPs that have fled Boko Haram.

In FY 2014 and FY 2015, the United States is providing nearly $25 million in humanitarian assistance in support of aid groups who are providing essential protection and emergency assistance to refugees, IDPs, and other populations of concern affected by Boko Haram in Cameroon, Chad, Niger, and Nigeria. We are continually assessing the situation and are committed to providing a robust response to emerging needs. In addition, the United States is engaging with the Government of Nigeria regarding ways to increase and improve its operational capacity to assist IDPs within the country.

Question. Turning to the Sahel region, the 2015 Omnibus appropriation included $3 million for social, educational, and vocational programs to assist former slaves in Mauritania, Mali, and Senegal to reintegrate into society. Can you elaborate on plans for these appropriated funds?

Answer. We plan to continue our whole-of-government approach to the range of actions required: assisting freed slaves to gain livelihood skills; pressing for identification of slaves, their liberation, and prosecution of slaveowners; and supporting the action plan adopted by the government to eradicate the practice.

We will direct this funding towards support for the reintegration and advancement of ex-slaves through an expansion of our existing vocational education programs. Lack of marketable skills or viable livelihood alternatives prevents many ex-slaves from leaving the service of their former masters. We would expand the scope of our existing judicial programs beyond the current counterterrorism focus to include support for judicial reform and education to assist slaves to obtain their freedom, to hold slaveowners accountable, and to procure civil status documentation for former slaves, which is required to access their full rights as citizens, including voting rights.

Question. Turning to the Sahel region, the 2015 Omnibus appropriation included $3 million for social, educational, and vocational programs to assist former slaves in Mauritania, Mali, and Senegal to reintegrate into society. How does the U.S. Government engage with and support abolitionist groups in the Sahel—particularly in Mauritania, Mali, Senegal, and Niger?

Answer. The United States view is well known in Mauritania: all sectors of society—to include government, civil society, and religious leaders—must work together to end the practice of slavery, as well as related social ills that developed over several centuries. Some recent examples of our efforts to implement this goal include:

—In December 2014, the Ambassador hosted a 5-hour meeting of ruling party members and representatives of three antislavery NGOs (El Hor, SOS–Esclaves, and IRA) to seek improved cooperation in eradicating slavery.
—We focus our limited humanitarian assistance and even more limited development assistance funding on freed-slave communities and other marginalized groups.
—We also routinely discuss with American investors how their firms can be helpful in suppressing slavery and improving the lives of former slaves.

In Niger, as part of ongoing dialogue with government and civil society and in research for annual reports on human rights and TIP, our Embassy in Niamey speaks with entities active against TIP and traditional slavery, including Association Timidria, a well-known Nigerien NGO, and invites members to events.

In Senegal, the United States supports abolitionist groups through our antitrafficking programming, including the $750,000 Plan International project, "Addressing Children's Basic Rights in Senegal." This project conducts training for legal system personnel on the identification of trafficking victims and the application of antitrafficking legislation, developing a standard national referral system for trafficking victims, and working with communities to raise awareness of trafficking and develop community-based mechanisms in response.

Question. What is the U.S. Government doing to raise concerns about recent crackdowns in Mauritania against abolitionist activists, Biram Dah Abeid, Brahim Ramdhane (President and Vice President of the Initiative for the Resurgence of the Abolitionist Movement in Mauritania), and Djibi Sow (President of Kawal e Yelitaare), who were sentenced to 2 years in prison on January 15, 2015, for disturbing public order and being members of an unregistered organization?

Answer. We repeatedly urge the appellate court to review the convictions and sentencing without delay, and to handle these important cases in a fair, impartial, and transparent manner. We communicated this message in press statements and other media engagements. We have spoken directly to all of Mauritania's senior government leadership, including the President, Prime Minister, Foreign Minister, Justice Minister and Members of Parliament, about our intense interest in these three cases. We have spoken to a wide range of political, religious and business leaders about these cases and the pending appeal.

Question. In 2014, Mauritania approved a "Roadmap to Combat the Consequences of Slavery," and created a special tribunal to prosecute cases of slavery. However, since its creation, the tribunal has not prosecuted a single case of slavery, and local reports suggest that it is underresourced. What is the U.S. Government doing, if anything, to assist Mauritania with the implementation of the "Roadmap" and the successful operation of the tribunal?

Answer. We work closely with the Mauritanian Government and civil society to implement the "Roadmap," including establishment of the special tribunal. We urged government and civil society to work together on implementing the "Roadmap" through our frequent high level engagements with senior host government and civil society leaders and through our public appeals in the Mauritanian media. We brought together government and civil society leaders to review and improve on their cooperation to implement the "Roadmap."

One aspect of the "Roadmap" involves improving social and economic conditions of former slaves and their descendants. The USG is supporting civil society's to engage on these issues. The Minister of Justice and the Solicitor General have committed to appointing judges to the new special tribunal who come from the community of slave descendants so that they will be especially attuned to handle these cases appropriately.

RESPONSES OF SARAH SEWALL TO QUESTIONS
SUBMITTED BY SENATOR MARCO RUBIO

Question. On February 10, I sent a letter to President Obama requesting that he appoint a qualified individual to the position of Ambassador At Large to Monitor and Combat Trafficking in Persons, which has been vacant since November of last year. This post oversees the State Department's Trafficking in Person's Office as well as the composition of the annual Trafficking in Persons Report.

◆ When do you believe this post will be filled?
◆ What impact does the vacancy of this position have on the U.S.'s efforts to combat trafficking?
◆ What steps have you taken to make sure that the TIP office will have the political clout to prevail in internal discussions at the State Department on tier rankings and other TIP report content?

Answer. The Department is working closely with the White House on this as we all hope to see a new Ambassador at Large nominated and confirmed to lead the Office to Monitor and Combat Trafficking in Persons as soon as possible. In the interim, the President, Secretary Kerry, and the entire Obama administration are committed to combat human trafficking.

The State Department has dedicated staff working on human trafficking issues in Washington, DC, and at each U.S. Embassy around the world. These dedicated staff will continue to advance the United States unwavering commitment to combat this crime through diplomacy and programming. We will also produce a Trafficking in Persons Report that accurately reflects government efforts to address the crime of trafficking in person.

For nearly 15 years, the TIP Report has galvanized international efforts to prosecute traffickers, protect victims, and prevent the crime from occurring in the first place.

Question. One of the only enforcement mechanisms the U.S. Government has against countries who perform poorly in combating human trafficking is to restrict nonhumanitarian and nontrade related foreign aid from countries who receive a Tier 3 ranking in the annual Trafficking in Persons Report.

◆ How effective have these sanctions or threat of sanctions been at encouraging states to increase their antitrafficking efforts?
◆ What other tools can the U.S. Government use to encourage states to attempt to meet the standards set forth by the TVPA?

Answer. The TIP Report shines a spotlight on the deficiencies in a country's antitrafficking efforts. The publicity around this report, accompanied by Tier 3 designations for countries not making significant efforts to fully comply with minimum standards for eliminating trafficking, is one of the most powerful tools we have to encourage improved efforts. Generally, the rankings themselves help hold governments accountable and motivate them to develop policies and structures to fight this crime. There is a correlation between tier ranking downgrades and states' subsequent enactment of anti-trafficking legislation.

Other available and powerful tools include ongoing diplomatic engagement, foreign assistance programming, and multilateral diplomacy. U.S. officials engage foreign government officials regularly to encourage progress on recommendations in the TIP Report. U.S. assistance programs help build capacity for government and nongovernment entities to combat human trafficking in their own countries. Public diplomacy initiatives help raise awareness. The United States continues to work with our partners around the world to prosecute and convict more traffickers, identify and protect more victims, and better prevent this crime.

Question. Trafficking of domestic workers by diplomats is a major issue around the world, including in the United States. There have been a number of high profile cases of diplomats perpetrating severe forms of labor exploitation against their domestic workers, including forced labor/human trafficking.

♦ What is the State Department doing to mitigate these risks?

Answer. The fair treatment of domestic workers employed by foreign mission personnel in the United States is a matter of great importance, and the Department of State is committed to protecting the welfare of these domestic workers, both to prevent abuse of these workers and to address allegations of mistreatment when they arise. The Department's commitment is reflected in a series of measures implemented over the past few years to provide increased safeguards for domestic workers.

The Department periodically sends out circular notes to the diplomatic community reminding chiefs of mission of the requirements for employing domestic workers, including that foreign missions must "pre-notify" the Department of any prospective domestic worker before the worker can be issued a visa. Our process ensures that mission leadership is aware of all domestic workers in the employ of mission personnel.

Wage payments to domestic workers must take the form of noncash payments directly to the worker—either by check or electronic transfer into a bank account in the domestic worker's name—starting after 90 days of the commencement of their employment. Prior to the domestic worker being granted a visa, foreign mission personnel employing the domestic worker enter into a written contract that covers duties, hours of work, minimum wage (which must be the greater of the minimum wage under U.S. federal and state law or the prevailing wage), overtime, and transportation (to and from the United States at commencement and termination of employment must be paid by the employer). The contract must be written in both English and if the domestic worker does not understand English, a language understood by the domestic worker. The contract must also specify that travel documents, such as a passport, must remain in the sole possession of the domestic worker. Employment and payment records must be retained for 3 years after the termination of employment. In addition, the Department prohibits deductions from wages for food and lodging.

U.S. consular officers abroad are required to interview domestic workers applying for visas and are trained to look for indicators of human trafficking. Consular officers also are required to confirm that all domestic worker visa applicants have received, read, and understand the "Know Your Rights" pamphlet, which provides information on the domestic workers' rights pertaining to their employment, signs of human trafficking, an overview of the nonimmigrant visa process, and the telephone number for the National Human Trafficking Resource Center hotline, which supports multilanguage needs.

Working with interagency partners, the Department of State led the creation of a Wilberforce video summarizing the information in the "Know Your Rights" pamphlet and translated it into 12 languages. The video was released in April 2014 and is played in consular waiting rooms around the world.

The Department of State takes seriously any allegation of domestic worker abuse, and has established a Trafficking in Persons Unit within the Bureau of Diplomatic Security's Criminal Investigations Division. This unit works closely with the Department of Justice's Human Trafficking Prosecutions Unit as well as with other federal law enforcement agencies involved in human trafficking investigations.

We would be glad to provide a briefing on other steps we take to prevent abuse of domestic workers.

Question. We have received credible reports that India is attempting to get around the protections in the TVPA for A–3/G–5 domestic workers by misclassifying these workers as A–2 visa program eligible, and that the Department of State is issuing these A–2 visas allowing this misclassification.

- ♦ Is this true? Please provide this committee with a list of visas granted under the A–2 program for India.
- ♦ If it's not true, what are you doing to ensure that this does NOT happen?

Answer. The Department works to ensure that the individuals who come to the United States in the personal employ of, and working in the private residences of, mission members as domestic workers enter the United States with an A–3 or G–5 visa. The legal requirements for A–3 visas, which are for domestic workers, are different than the requirements for A–2 visas. A visa applicant may be issued an A–2 visa only if he or she meets all requirements for A–2 visa issuance. Broadly speaking, A–2 is a visa category for foreign government employees performing official activities for a foreign government. All visa applications are adjudicated by consular officers based on their individual merits. We are happy to provide further briefings, although we cannot discuss specific visa cases.

Question. In 2008, Congress passed the William Wilberforce Trafficking Victims Protection Reauthorization Act, Public Law 110–457. That law included a provision, "Section 203(a)(2), requiring the Secretary of State to suspend the issuance of A–3 or G–5 visas to applicants "seeking to work for officials of a diplomatic mission or an international organization, if the Secretary determines that there is credible evidence that one or more employees" have abused or exploited one or more non-immigrants holding an A–3 or G–5 visa, where the diplomatic mission or international organization has tolerated such actions." Despite numerous cases of trafficking by diplomats, the State Department has yet to use this tool.

- ♦ Is the State Department considering suspending India or any other countries from the A–3/G–5 visa program who have displayed the clear pattern of exploitation of domestic workers? If not, why not?

Answer. Although there has not yet been a case of formal visa suspension under the William Wilberforce Act, the Department believes that the law has proven to have a significant deterrent value. For example, the law has been a factor in persuading foreign governments that they and their diplomats need to settle civil cases brought by former domestic workers. It also appears to have increased the general willingness of foreign missions to cooperate with U.S. investigations into alleged abuse and to take steps to ensure compliance with U.S. requirements relating to the employment of domestic workers. The Department will continue to review every allegation of domestic worker abuse that is brought to its attention and will take appropriate action in light of this review.

The Department encourages law enforcement authorities to investigate allegations of abuse of domestic workers to the fullest extent possible.

Question. As part of the Federal Strategic Action Plan on Services for Victims of Human Trafficking in the United States for 2013–2017, the State Department is supposed to develop procedures for in-person registration of domestic workers employed by diplomatic personnel in Washington DC. It is now 2015 and those interviews have not begun.

- ♦ What is the status of these procedures? When will the interview program be launched? Why was the original program shrunk from a national interview program to a "pilot" in Washington, DC, only? When will interviews be conducted on a national basis?

Answer. While the Department's initiative to implement annual in-person registration of domestic workers is well underway, the development involved additional resources, budgetary discussions, and the need for the system to be conducive for the majority of non-English speaking domestic workers employed by foreign diplomatic personnel. We will begin in-person registration of domestic workers in the Washington, DC, area, which has the highest number of workers employed by foreign mission personnel, this summer. Once this program is fully operational in Washington, the project will be implemented in New York City followed by other cities throughout the United States. This effort will serve as an important tool to prevent abuse and will provide domestic workers an avenue in which they may raise to the Department matters of concern related to their employment. Prior to the roll-out of the registration system, the Office of the Chief of Protocol will be holding a briefing for foreign mission deputy chiefs of mission regarding this new requirement, as well as a separate briefing for domestic workers (without their employers present) to discuss domestic workers rights and responsibilities, and available resources in the event of abuse or mistreatment.

Question. The State Department has also failed to follow up with annual briefings for domestic workers and their diplomatic employers in New York and Washington, DC.

♦ When will these briefing sessions be convened? Why have these meetings not been held on an annual basis?

Answer. The Department is committed to combating trafficking in persons and continues to conduct briefings for representatives of the diplomatic corps to inform them of current requirements regarding the employment of domestic workers and to underscore that it is essential that we continue our joint efforts to ensure all domestic workers understand their rights and protections and that those employing them understand their contract obligations and their responsibilities. The last such briefing for diplomatic corps representatives was held in early summer 2014 and the next briefing is being scheduled for early summer 2015.

A briefing for domestic workers will be held in summer 2015. At that time, the workers will be advised of the new annual in-person registration requirement.

www.ingramcontent.com/pod-product-compliance
Lightning Source LLC
Chambersburg PA
CBHW081226280526
45787CB00006B/2544

* 9 7 8 1 5 1 8 8 4 7 8 5 1 *